Sunset

Easy-Care Gardening

By the Editors of Sunset Books and Sunset Magazine

Trunks of Melaleuca quinquenervia *rise from drifts of pink and white* Impatiens; *pots contain white* Catharanthus roseus.

Lane Publishing Co. • Menlo Park, California

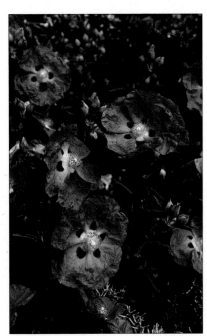

Luminous blossoms of orchid rockrose,
Cistus purpureus.

Research & Text
Philip Edinger

Developmental Editor
Karen Hewitt

Coordinating Editor
Cornelia Fogle

Contributing Editor
Phyllis Elving

Design
Joe di Chiarro

Cover: Simple garden layout features uncluttered expanses of brick paving and
lawn; shrubs and trees form permanent
planting framework. Most seasonal color
stems from annuals in easy-to-care-for
narrow beds and raised planter. Design
by Williams & Ziller Design. Photography
by Tom Wyatt. Photo styling by JoAnn
Masaoka.

Photographers

Glenn Christiansen: page 19. **Derek Fell:**
pages 28, 40, 42 bottom, 44 bottom left,
48, 55, 56, 58, 59, 62, 63, 70, 73, 75, 78.
Gerald R. Fredrick: page 52 bottom.
Mark E. Gibson: page 25. **Horticultural
Photography:** pages 31, 32, 33 bottom, 66,
76. **Steve W. Marley:** page 22 top left. **Ells
Marugg:** pages 22 bottom left, 27, 33 top,
36, 49, 68 top, 71. **JoAnn Masaoka:** pages
9, 21 bottom. **Bill Ross:** page 23. **Teri
Sandison:** pages 37 bottom, 64 bottom
right. **Jeff Teeter:** page 2. **Michael S.
Thompson:** pages 3, 29, 41, 44 top right,
46, 51, 53 top, 60 top left, 68 bottom left.
Darrow M. Watt: page 52 top right. **Tom
Wyatt:** pages 1, 4, 6, 7, 8, 10, 13, 14, 15, 16,
20, 21 top, 24, 34, 37 top, 42 top, 50, 52
left, 54, 60 bottom right, 61, 79, 80, 83, 84,
87, 89, 90, 93. **Elisabet Zeilon:** page 39.

Photo stylist: **JoAnn Masaoka:** pages 1, 4,
6, 7, 8, 10, 13, 14, 15, 16, 20, 21 top, 22 top
left, 24, 34, 37 top, 42 top, 50, 52 left, 54,
60 bottom right, 61, 79, 80, 83, 84, 87, 89,
90, 93.

Editor, Sunset Books: Elizabeth L. Hogan

Second printing February 1989

Carefree Gardening

The desire for a good-looking garden
is as strong today as ever. But more
and more activities seem to be making demands on our leisure time,
leaving us with less and less time for
garden care. The challenge is raised:
How can traditional gardening methods and materials be re-evaluated so
that a satisfying garden can be maintained with less effort?

To answer this challenge, *Easy-
Care Gardening* takes you through
each step of the planning that is at
the heart of "easy care," from evaluation of site potential to actual installation—always with an eye toward
maintenance time. We offer detailed
descriptions of a great number of
plants that are easy to grow and need
little maintenance to remain attractive and healthy. And we suggest the
labor-saving tools, watering aids,
and common-sense attention that
round out the easy-care concept.

For their help in manuscript preparation, we thank landscape architect
E. Parker Smith of Sebastopol, CA;
landscape designer Gary J. Patterson
of Cloverdale, CA; and horticulturists Richard Goula of Lafayette, LA,
Bruce Keeney of Fort Plain, NY, John
C. MacGregor IV of South Pasadena,
CA, and Roger Nelson of Wayne, NE.

For sharing materials for photography, we thank Growers Supply
and Irrigation and Menlo Park Hardware Co. Finally, we acknowledge
the contribution of copy editor
Rebecca La Brum, who attended
to clarity, precision, and grace of
content.

Contents

Clump of Hosta undulata *'Variegata' is backed by dark leaves of* Acer palmatum *'Ornatum'; behind is pink-flowered* Cornus florida.

Special Features

Easy Care...
The Possible Dream

*H*ave you ever wondered how some people have time for tennis or golf, frequent weekend travel, and relaxing hobbies—yet still have attractive gardens? Do they have 10 green thumbs, or an invisible crew of gardeners?

Fortunately for you, neither of these is likely to be true (though a green thumb always helps). Your envied neighbors have simply mastered the concept of easy-care gardening: they've learned that a lovely garden need not make a slave of its owner. You *can* have a garden that looks great yet leaves you free to pursue other interests.

A commitment to easy-care gardening does not mean converting your yard to concrete and crushed rock, nor does it mean surrounding yourself with the monotonous verdure of a freeway landscape. An easy-care garden is simply one that meets your needs but demands no more time than you're willing to give. As long as it satisfies this requirement, the garden can have any style you choose.

All successful easy-care gardens do have one thing in common, though: they begin with a careful, well-thought-out plan. And that's the key to easy-care gardening: *plan before you act.* To keep your property looking good with a minimal investment of time, choose an efficient design and easy-care plants, and establish time-saving routines. On pages 22 to 78, you'll find descriptions of proven easy-care plants; review pages 80 to 94 for tips on garden care.

Large, easy-care surfaces of brick and unobstructed lawn make up most of this garden (shown on cover); container plants and a narrow bed of annuals provide color.

Developing an Easy-Care Garden

Easy-care gardening has a twofold goal: to reduce maintenance time and to ensure that the time spent is as pleasurable as possible. Another objective, of course, is personal satisfaction—an easy-care garden, like any other, should have an appearance you enjoy.

In planning your garden, begin with some careful evaluation. If you're starting from scratch, what maintenance pitfalls should you be sure to avoid? If you're redesigning your garden, what problems need to be remedied? In contemplating a makeover, it's also important to determine whether you need to tackle the entire property or just part of it. Sometimes the chief high-care problem—a large, demanding lawn, for example—can be isolated and remedied without touching the rest of the yard.

Next, decide what you want from your garden besides an easy maintenance routine. What should it look like? What will its functions be?

Uncluttered design *with a restrained choice of different plants showcases a specimen flowering cherry,* Prunus yedoensis *'Akebono'.*

The third step is to analyze your site. Determine how its features and limitations affect your "dream garden"—and adjust your plans accordingly. Finally, move on to the actual design of the garden, choosing plants and structural materials that appeal to you and suit the site.

Evaluating Your Garden

In general, those extra hours of garden care can be traced to one or more of the following five problem areas. As you plan your garden, these are the pitfalls to be aware of.

Poor garden design. An inefficient layout can add hours to the maintenance routine.

Look closely at the circulation patterns. Does foot traffic flow through the garden as you'd like? The best, most frequently used path to the front door shouldn't run straight across the lawn. Do you have easy access to areas that need routine care? Pathways and entryways should be large enough to accommodate necessary equipment; planting beds shouldn't be so deep that you can't easily reach the plants and soil in the center or back.

Lawns. No other part of the standard garden generates more complaints than does the lawn. A special headache is often the front lawn, groomed and preened for public show but offering little pleasure to the gardener. Ask yourself if the rewards of a showpiece lawn are really worth the effort. If the answer to this question is "no," you might consider replacing the lawn with a ground cover that demands less care or putting the lawn space to a more satisfying use—an enclosed patio, for example.

If you do want a lawn, choose a grass or grass mixture that's suited to your climate. Trying to coax good performance from an unsuitable type adds time and frustration to the maintenance regime.

Is the layout of your lawn simple and uncluttered? Irregular or sharply angled borders make mowing and edging more time-consuming, as do trees, shrubs, or planting beds in the midst of the turf.

Do you have mowing strips? These borders of brick or concrete separate lawn from flower beds, making the lawn edges much easier to mow. Mowing strips also keep grass from encroaching on (and having to be pulled from) the soil of the beds.

Inappropriate plants. If you choose plants that just aren't right for your garden, no amount of care will make them perform as you'd like.

(Continued on page 9)

Flowing surface of aged brick paving needs no upkeep beyond periodic sweeping, leaving maintenance time free for mixed plantings of perennials and shrubs.

Strong Oriental design motif achieves easy-care status with expanses of decking and paving, and attractive but limited planting areas.

Professional Help At Your Service

I f you lack the time, energy, or inspiration to tackle the design or installation of your easy-care garden, you'll probably need to enlist professional help for the project. In the Yellow Pages of your telephone directory, you'll find listings for all the services you may need.

Before hiring any professional service, ask for references if you are not already familiar with the company's work. Also expect to sign a contract spelling out precisely what services will be provided.

Landscape architects have a college or university degree in landscape architecture and/or a license certifying successful completion of the Uniform National Examination in Landscape Architecture. Many states require that landscape architects have a license to practice.

These professionals can prepare a garden design that includes all or some of the following: overall design, grading plan, irrigation plan, construction details, planting plan. Many landscape architects provide consultations (for a fee) to determine the extent of services required.

Landscape designers can prepare an overall garden design and planting plan but, in contrast to landscape architects, they aren't licensed and may or may not have had formal education in the field. Given this lack of professional regulation, their expertise may vary widely; the best of them may have worked with a licensed professional or received formal training in landscape architecture (though they lack a degree).

Landscape contractors are trained to install landscapes; in many states, they must be licensed.

In addition to handling soil preparation, grading, and planting, a landscape contractor can install water systems (some will design them as well) and install or subcontract structural work such as decks, fences, retaining walls, and walkways.

When you sign a contract for specified services, be sure it states that the design will be followed. The contract should also specify a completion date and contain a statement of liability. If the contract doesn't specify coverage for injury or property damage, be sure that the contractor is covered for such damages. At the very least, make certain you're protected by homeowner's insurance or some other policy.

Water systems contractors. If you need help only with the design and/or installation of a water system, engage a landscape contractor or look in the Yellow Pages under "Sprinklers–Garden & Lawn, Installation & Service."

Structural contractors. Though a landscape contractor may be able to perform the structural work your plan calls for, you may prefer to engage individuals specializing in particular fields: carpenters or building contractors, fencing contractors, masonry contractors.

Planting help. To install an entire landscape, you'll need the help of a landscape contractor. But if you simply want some extra muscle for a few hours of planting, a good retail nursery may be able to recommend a responsible gardener.

Professional design guidance transformed a humdrum hillside into a waterfall and a sweep of shrubs leading to a rustic pool. Landscape design: Kathryn Mathewson Associates.

Flowering lily-of-the-Nile (Agapanthus) *stands out in a landscape of plants chosen to thrive with moderate water and minimal attention. Dry streambed conceals a natural drainage channel.*

. . . Evaluating Your Garden

Be sure to select plants that suit your climate and garden environment (see pages 22 to 78) and plant them where they'll grow well. Consider water, soil, wind, and light conditions; remember that trees and shrubs with greedy surface roots can make it difficult to grow other plants nearby. And try to avoid mixing plants with differing cultural requirements; if you treat them all alike (and if they're planted together, it's difficult not to), some will always perform poorly.

Equally troublesome are plants that grow *too* well—billowing over walkways, looming in front of windows. When you make your selections, keep in mind each plant's size at maturity.

Finally, if pests and diseases regularly afflict your favorite plants, you should consider choosing new favorites. It's a constant battle to keep problem-prone plants looking good.

Inadequate preparation. Even the best design won't save you time if you overlook preparatory work. Evaluate the soil *before* you plant. Will it support a garden as is, or do you need to make improvements before setting in your plants?

What are the natural drainage patterns in your yard? You may need to do some grading to redirect water or add downspouts or other diversions so rainwater won't cascade into flower beds or wash over pathways.

Is it easy to water all areas of the garden well? If not, consider installing a built-in watering system; it can be a real time saver for you. Another solution, of course, is to lay out your garden so moisture-loving plants aren't located in those hard-to-reach areas.

Underestimated maintenance. It's not unusual to know what chores need to be done, yet have little idea of how long the work will take. A crucial part of evaluating your old garden—and planning your new one—is a careful review of anticipated maintenance.

Make a complete list of all the routine care your garden requires, including weekly as well as once- or twice-yearly chores. Then, as best you can, tally the hours per week or month you spend (or expect to spend) on each task. If the total strikes you as too high, adjust your garden design and plant choices until you've reduced the hours of labor to your satisfaction.

Your Ideal Garden

Whether you're creating a completely new garden or redesigning all or part of an existing one, one of your first steps will be to make a "wish list." What do you envision for your ideal garden?

Simple streetside planting presents a neat, attractive face for public view, while concealing a private patio for owners' outdoor enjoyment.

Private space in front yard shows how easily screen plantings (above) can form a tranquil oasis just feet from a busy street.

Function. At the outset, decide what your garden's function should be. Do you want a public show-place or a private spot screened from passersby and neighbors? Or perhaps you'd like both public and private areas. For example, if the garden will be used for entertaining or family barbecues, you'll want at least part of it secluded from view.

If the garden's function is likely to change in the future, try to plan for alternative uses from the start. A children's play area can be adapted for grown-up pastimes later on—you might install a pool or spa, or cover the area with a deck or ground cover.

Seasonal needs. Ask yourself how you'll use the garden throughout the year. Are you content with more or less the same look from month to month, or do you want seasonal variety? Are you regularly away from home at any time of year? If you're typically gone during summer, for example, you may not want a lush lawn and summer-flowering plants, but you'll almost certainly need an auto-mated watering system.

Maintenance goals. How much maintenance are you willing to do? That's one question to answer at the start. If you have little interest in gardening or little time for it, your goal will be to streamline care in every way possible: install an automated water-ing system; make use of mulches and/or herbi-cides to cut down on weeds; simplify the lawn design; or replace the grass with a deck, paving, or a ground cover.

On the other hand, if gardening is one of your hobbies, you may want to shape your plans around a passion for growing roses, irises, or vege-tables. Or perhaps you'd like to devote available time to a showpiece area of seasonal color. In these cases, you might set up the greater portion of the landscape for easy care—and lavish your spare time on your pet plants.

If you do plan to incorporate a special interest into an overall easy-care scheme, it's likely that it will influence the garden design. For example, the one hot, sunny area of your property may have to be devoted to your prize tomatoes, since that's the only spot where they'll flourish. As you plan, though, be sure that the needs of your hobby plants don't interfere with your overall easy-care goals.

It's also important to decide what *types* of main-tenance you want to emphasize. Note your least favorite chores—lawn-mowing, watering, edg-ing—and make a concerted effort to plan a garden that reduces the time you spend at those particular tasks. Likewise, note the jobs you don't mind (or that you actually enjoy), then see that your garden will feature these.

Analyzing Your Site

Once you've decided what you want in your easy-care garden, take a good look at your property. Consider how its features and the regional condi-tions will affect your plans.

Consider the climate

The garden you plan must be in harmony with the local climate: summer heat and winter cold, annual rainfall patterns, winds, seasonal humidity, cloud or fog cover.

An easy-care garden will often emphasize native plants and those from very similar climates, but your choices are by no means limited to these plants, since conditions can be adjusted to some extent (through supplemental watering, for exam-ple). As always, though, keep ease of care in mind: don't select any plant that requires too much alter-ation of the environment.

Sun & shade. Where should you locate a patio or barbecue? Which plants are best for which loca-tions? To answer these questions intelligently, you need to determine the sun/shade patterns on your property.

First, note how the sun strikes your yard throughout the day. Determine which parts of your garden will be on the sunny sides of struc-tures, which in the shade. Do you have large trees that cast shade on their western sides in the morn-ing, on their eastern sides in the afternoon? Are there tall buildings, hills, or mountains nearby that prolong morning shade or hasten the onset of shadows?

Also be aware that light patterns change from season to season. The sun rises higher in summer than in winter, so some parts of the garden may be sunny in summer, shaded during colder months.

Wind. Wind patterns are less predictable than sun and shade, but they're no less a factor in garden planning. Note wind directions and windy times of year. If you're new to the area, ask local resi-dents about typical wind character; look at mature trees and windbreaks for a "lean" that indicates wind direction and intensity. Again, your findings will influence plant selection and placement of rec-reation areas, and determine the possible need for windbreaks.

Water. Virtually all gardens need more water than nature provides. Before working out your garden plans, determine the availability and cost of water. Where water is costly or in limited supply, choose drought-tolerant plants and consider installing an economical low-volume water delivery system and a controller (see pages 85 to 88).

Test the soil

The nature of your garden soil—sand, clay, or loam (see page 83), acid or alkaline—determines which plants are best suited to your garden. Soil depth and compaction will also influence your plans.

If you want to grow deep-rooted plants, a shallow soil—one overlying bedrock or a thick hardpan layer—almost dictates a garden featuring raised beds. Soil that has been compacted by heavy equipment may yield to loosening by a landscape contractor, but again, raised beds filled with imported, good soil may be the simplest, least expensive solution.

Drainage. As important as soil type (and closely linked to it) is drainage—the movement of water through the soil. Sandy soils drain quickly, clay and compacted soil slowly; loam falls somewhere in between. If your garden drains more rapidly in some areas than in others, you may need to loosen or amend the soil in those slow-draining spots.

Runoff. Water runoff depends not only on soil type but also on the locations of buildings on the property and on whether the land is sloping or level. During rainy periods, observe the natural flow of water, both as it falls on open ground and as it runs off structures and out of drainpipes. Will you need to divert any of this flow by grading or trenching? If your yard drains slowly in general, you should be certain to construct all pathways a bit above grade so water will run off to the surrounding ground.

Other considerations

If you have power or telephone lines above your property, you'll know to leave that airspace free of tree limbs or structures.

It's also important to know precisely where any underground utility lines and septic installations are placed—and to note how deeply they're buried. You don't want to disturb any of these structures during construction, and you may want to leave open ground above them if there's any chance that future maintenance or repair will require excavation. Also leave easy access to all utility meters and any cleanout inlets to your home's main drain.

Be sure to note the placement of all hose bibbs. Though they can be moved, it's a good idea to see if you can work the existing locations into your plans.

Off-site influences. You may find you need to muffle persistent noise or screen unscenic views from the garden. Noise from a nearby highway or industry can be diffused and deflected by thick plantings and/or walls; unsightly views are often easily dealt with by careful shrub or tree placement or by fencing.

Other restrictions. Always be sure to learn what, if any, legal restrictions apply to construction or landscaping on your property. See if your deed mentions easements that must remain open or other limitations. Then check city or county ordinances. Fence height limitations and setbacks on secondary structures are the two statutes most commonly affecting landscape planning, but some communities also have codes specifying that only approved structural materials or colors can be used for walls and fences. A call to city or county offices will let you know if you need permits for any of the work you're planning.

Finally, don't overlook your neighbors' opinions. If you're planning to make significant (though technically permissible) changes to the landscape, inform your neighbors and consider their reactions.

Choosing Your Garden's Appearance

As you consider the ideal look for your garden, keep several points in mind. First, of course, let the limitations of your site guide you: a woodsy backyard expanse of redwoods and pines is clearly not feasible if your lot is only 20 feet square. Beyond this, though, you'll want to aim for overall harmony between the garden and its surroundings.

Garden design & plant choices. When you evaluate different garden designs, you'll be guided by intended garden uses and your low-maintenance goals. At the same time, though, be sure to think about how each design coordinates with the architecture of your house. Avoid incongruous combinations—for example, a desert-style landscape of cacti, succulents, and rocks is clearly the wrong choice for an English Tudor–style home.

Also, make sure that the plants you choose fit the design of the garden: a geometrically rigid layout would not be the best setting for tropical plants.

Materials. The building materials used in your garden, whether brick, stone, wood, or concrete, should harmonize with the appearance of the house (see "General guidelines" on page 15). Another hallmark of good garden style is limited

Repeated use of a few different plants emphasizes this home's strong architecture. Bedding begonias provide masses of quick color between slow-growing shrubs. Landscape design: Robert Duranleau.

Taking its theme from native plants, this desert landscape gets shade from palo verde (Cercidium floridum). Strong structural elements are in harmony with the surrounding terrain. Landscape architect: Carol Shuler.

use of different materials in the same garden. Remember: less variety in materials leads to greater design harmony.

Putting Your Plans on Paper

After you've settled on the sort of garden that suits your site and your preferences, you're ready to put your plans on paper. An accurate site plan allows you to experiment with design, lay out water systems, sketch in decks and other structures, and plan circulation patterns and planting beds—all without even lifting a shovel.

Creating a site plan

If you have a deed map or house plans from the developer or architect, you may find a drawing that shows your house situated on its lot with many dimensions given. In this case, double check some of the figures, especially those giving the distance from house to property lines. If they're reliable, use them to draw your own working plan.

Taking the measurements. Measure and sketch the house outline on paper, noting all dimensions. Also indicate the positions, sizes, and height from the ground of all doors and windows. Indicate the locations of all overhead and underground utility lines, noting their respective height and depth from ground level; also mark the placement of utility meters, cleanouts, and hose bibbs.

Measure to the property lines from a base line (it's easiest to use one side of the house) and note these distances on the sketch. Then measure to any other structures, walks, and driveways that will remain in your new garden plan. Measure each structure; establish its base line and note its position on the property. Also measure to (and indicate on your sketch) any trees, plants, or planting beds that you intend to keep.

Graphing your garden design

Using the raw data from your sketch, you can create a base plan on graph paper. Choose a ¼-inch or ⅛-inch grid; either size will let you draw a plan that's large enough to work on comfortably, yet not so big that you need to spread it on a banquet table.

Harmonious design *for easy care: divider wall and decking repeat the wood of the house siding; rectangular shapes prevail in layout of structures and understated garden. Landscape design: Page Sanders.*

Using the measurements from your site sketch, neatly draw in the property lines, utility lines, all structures, and all plants you will keep. Draw in arrows to indicate the direction of sloping land; note the top and bottom of each slope. And finally, include an arrow that indicates north. When all of these elements are on paper, you have a working base plan to use while laying out your garden.

Because the design process involves several steps—and you'll no doubt change your mind as you go along—you'll want to preserve your base plan unaltered. There are several simple ways to do this. You can do all your designing on tracing paper or acetate overlaying the base plan; or simply make photocopies of the base plan or have it duplicated by a blueprint firm.

Structural plans. Referring to your base plan for the locations of all the inalterable elements on your property, design your structural additions. These should include both the utilitarian and the recreational—decks, overheads, planters or raised beds, walks, fences, and storage areas. This is your chance to organize circulation patterns that can later ease your maintenance tasks. Also visualize walking through the garden; this will help you get the feel of the space you're creating.

While you design, think of the materials you want to use; as your design takes shape, you can calculate quantities and estimate their cost.

Planting plans. When you've firmed up the structural design, turn your attention to planting plans. In general, you can follow the same guidelines used for positioning garden structures: Will your proposed plantings interfere with sunlight or circulation? Will they block windows or desirable views? If there's a structure or a view you'd like to hide, can plants provide an effective screen?

Initially, just rough in general indications of the basic types of plants—trees, shrubs, perennials, ground covers—and their locations. Then, when you're comfortable with your design, you can approach the pleasant task of choosing specific plants. Referring to the base plan grid, indicate the spacing of plants, keeping in mind their size at maturity; from this, you can determine the number of plants you'll need and estimate their total cost.

Water system layout. Though a watering system is often installed before planting, it's best to plan your system *after* you've settled on a planting layout. Using the layout (and referring to your base plan for the location of water hookups), you can tailor a system to your specific needs—lawn, ground cover areas, mixed borders—using sprinklers, low-volume delivery systems, or a combination (see pages 85 to 89 for further information).

Harmony of home and garden: *Wood and concrete of house are repeated in garden structures. Simple landscape features Japanese maple (Acer palmatum) in a ground cover of English ivy (Hedera helix). Landscape design: Robert Duranleau.*

Choosing Structural Materials

Virtually every garden includes structural materials, though they may be nothing more elaborate than stepping stones or a concrete walkway. More often, the typical garden includes an assortment of structural elements, ranging from fences and walls to tool sheds and gazebos.

General guidelines

When choosing materials for garden structures, evaluate each one on the basis of its appearance, maintenance needs, and overall cost.

Broad expanses of tile *provide an easy-care surface in tones that harmonize with house and landscape boulders; angled walkways and pool design echo the tiles' square corners.*

Subtle details *coordinate house and garden structures. Brick paving repeats the decorative brick trim on the home's entry arch; the arch itself is echoed in the wooden arch spanning the pathway.*

Style. Building materials used in the garden should coordinate with your home's exterior. If you have a brick house, brick should be the prime candidate for pathways, steps, and planters. If, for variety or economy, you want to use a different material, use it in conjunction with the brick: an aggregate path with brick edging, for example, or a concrete planter with a brick cap.

Care. Find out what kind of care each material will need—and how often maintenance will be required. Is the material easy to clean? Will it degrade quickly? Will you need to apply (and reapply) paint and preservatives? Will weathering force parts out of alignment?

Cost. Always select the best materials you can afford. High-quality materials look better, last longer, and require less maintenance than cheaper ones. (It still pays to comparison-shop for the best price, though.)

In addition to the flat dollar cost of the material, factor in the expense involved in transporting heavy materials to your site and the cost of installation.

Which material for which structure?

Decks are almost always made of wood, but a variety of materials may be used for pavings, planters, fences, and other structures.

Decking & wood walks. Decay-resistant woods that age attractively, such as redwood, cedar, and cypress, are traditional choices for long-lived, trouble-free surfaces that age attractively. Pressure-treated lumber is a good (and often less expensive) alternative to naturally decay-resistant woods. And railroad ties, treated to resist rot, have found a variety of garden uses—chiefly as pathways, steps, retaining walls, and planters.

Remember, though, that "decay-resistant" does not mean "decay-proof." Any wood will decompose in time, especially if it's in contact with the ground.

Pavings, pathways, planters & walls. The most durable materials for contact with the ground are brick, concrete, tile, and stone. Beautiful and versatile, these materials make an almost infinite variety of patterns and designs possible. (Crushed rock and gravel pavings can be very attractive and are certainly inexpensive, but they do need regular maintenance.)

• *Brick* is a pleasing choice for planters, raised beds, fences, steps, and mowing strips. You can buy bricks in various sizes, dimensions, and colors, and set them either on a poured concrete base or in a bed of sand. Butted bricks or mortared joints are best, since weeds seem to gravitate to any spaces left between bricks.

• *Concrete* pavers and poured concrete both make durable steps, raised beds, and mowing strips. Concrete and pressure-treated wood are preferred materials for retaining walls. Poured concrete can conform to any shape; it may have a smooth, textured, or pebbled surface, and can even be stamped with special patterning tools to give the finished surface the look of stone, tile, or brick.

Concrete pavers, less expensive than brick, come in many colors and shapes; some are even interlocking. Install them as you would bricks.

• *Clay tile* makes a rustic yet elegant-looking paving that's as easy to lay as brick, though tiles are not as easily cut into smaller units. (If you decide on a tile pathway, remember that it will probably be slippery when wet.)

• *Stone* is best used as a paving surface, though it's possible to make New England–style stone fences and low retaining walls with stones that bed together snugly. Choose flagstone, slate, cobblestones, or river rocks; all are relatively simple to install in earth, sand, or concrete.

Selecting Easy-Care Plants

Choosing the perfect plants is perhaps the most important aspect of your garden design. After all, plants make the garden; and though all plants need some degree of attention, this is your chance to pick those that will thrive with a minimum of care.

On pages 22 to 78, you'll find listings for more than 120 easy-care plants. Many of these have gained that reputation because they perform well in a variety of climates and soils; others are easy-care in their native regions or in similar environments.

Any easy-care plant must be free from periodic debilitating or disfiguring attacks from pests and diseases, or at the very least, free from attack in most of the areas where it can be grown. The plants we recommend are relatively untroubled by pests and diseases; any significant regional problems are noted in the descriptions.

The easy-care plant should also have good garden manners—noninvasive growth and a noncompetitive root system—and should produce a minimum of litter. Finally, first-rate easy-care plants (aside from bulbs) should be naturally good-looking throughout the growing season. For this reason, our choices do not include plants requiring frequent pruning, thinning, or other attention to remain attractive.

Cultural considerations

When you're ready to choose the plants for your garden, begin by considering their cultural needs. Is your climate appropriate? Can you provide the necessary soil type, light conditions, and water?

Climate. Some plants are virtually carefree in a wide range of climates, while others perform well in particular conditions and fail miserably in others. Rhododendrons, for example, will flourish in cool, humid Seattle with almost no care, but in a hot, dry locale like Phoenix, they will be a tremendous challenge to grow. As you make your selections, pay attention to each plant's stated requirements and tolerances; if your climate doesn't offer what a plant needs, chances are it's not a good choice for your garden.

Climate zones. The plant hardiness zone map below, devised by the USDA, will help you determine which plants are right for your area. Zones on average expected low temperatures in winter; each zone encompasses a 10°F range.

To use the map, locate the hardiness zone in which you live. If the number listed with the plant description is the same or lower than your zone, then the plant should survive the winter temperatures. The zone listings indicate the range of climate zones for which each plant is adapted.

The map does, however, have some obvious limitations. Generally, a climate will extend over a large geographical area, but local modifications—such as altitude, slopes, and morning or evening shadow from mountains—create microclimates within the larger framework. In addition, such a map fails to acknowledge other significant factors that affect plant growth: humidity, expected high temperatures, soil types, and wind.

Fortunately, many plants will prosper in a variety of climates. But where significant limitations do exist, we have noted them (some plants aren't recommended for humid climates, for example) or

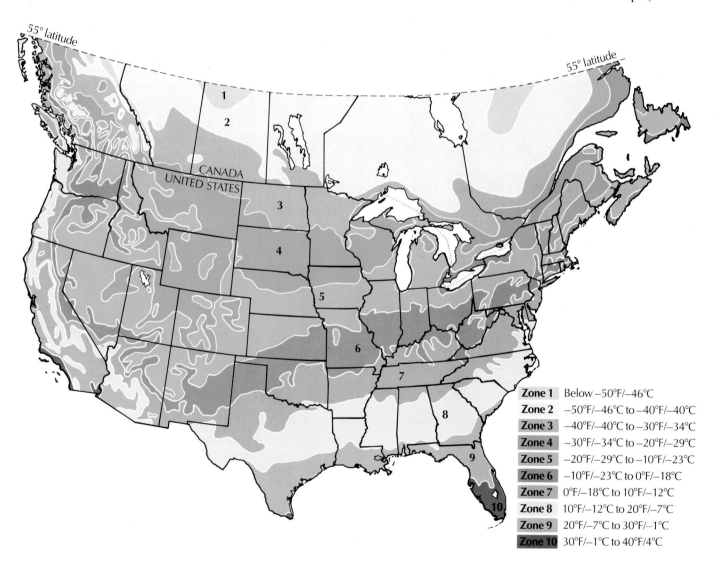

Zone 1	Below −50°F/−46°C
Zone 2	−50°F/−46°C to −40°F/−40°C
Zone 3	−40°F/−40°C to −30°F/−34°C
Zone 4	−30°F/−34°C to −20°F/−29°C
Zone 5	−20°F/−29°C to −10°F/−23°C
Zone 6	−10°F/−23°C to 0°F/−18°C
Zone 7	0°F/−18°C to 10°F/−12°C
Zone 8	10°F/−12°C to 20°F/−7°C
Zone 9	20°F/−7°C to 30°F/−1°C
Zone 10	30°F/−1°C to 40°F/4°C

indicated a different set of zones for eastern and western parts of the continent.

Exposure. Beyond knowing each plant's general climatic preferences, be aware of its requirements for sun and shade. In our listings, *sun* designates a plant that needs full sun all day long. Plants preferring *partial shade* do best in sunlight lightly filtered through a tree canopy or in spots receiving both sun and shade during the course of the day—sun in the morning, shade in the afternoon (or at least during the hottest part of the day). A preference for *shade* indicates a need for low light and relatively cool temperatures at all times.

Keep in mind, however, that each plant's preferred exposure is also determined by climate: full sun on the coast differs substantially from full desert sun. For this reason, you'll occasionally find different exposures recommended for different climates.

Soil. Many easy-care plants are as unparticular about soils as they are about climate. Pure sand and compacted clay or hardpan situations do offer special challenges, as do poorly drained soils or highly acid or alkaline types. But most garden soils are entirely suitable for many of our easy-care choices. Just be sure to determine your soil type when you analyze your site, then select plants that are sure performers in that situation. Alternatively, if the plants you want won't thrive in your soil, you can build raised beds and fill them with the proper soil type.

Soil requirements are listed with each plant description. Those designated *not particular* will grow in a wide range of soils—from light (sandy) to heavy (clay), somewhat acid (pH 6.5) to slightly alkaline (pH 7.2), slow- to fast-draining. If there is a special pH preference or extended tolerance, we indicate it with phrases such as *needs acid soil* or *tolerates alkaline soil.*

Needs well-drained soil applies to plants that won't prosper in soil that remains saturated for too long after a watering. Plants that *need good soil* require the sort of fertile, well-drained soil that can nourish a vegetable crop without any special preparation.

Water. A plant's water needs reflect the conditions found in its native environment. If you decide that you don't want to bother with regular watering, choose only native plants or those from very similar climates; they should flourish with only the water they receive from rain. However, you'll have much greater flexibility in plant choices if you're willing to establish a watering regime.

Water requirements are noted in the listing for each plant. Those few totally amenable types that will do well with any amount of water you give

The ultimate easy-care landscape uses only *plants that are native to the region. Natural rainfall meets watering needs; maintenance is limited to periodic grooming.*

them—from essentially none to a regular dose—are *not particular.* Plants that must have moisture at the root zone during the growing season *need regular watering. Needs moderate watering* indicates a plant that can take short periods of dryness in part of the root zone but that must have some carefully spaced watering during the growing season. Finally, some plants are *drought-tolerant.* A few of these must have dryness to do well; most, however, will also accept moderate watering. And some plants tolerate drought only under certain conditions—after root systems are established, for example, or in cool-summer climates.

If your garden is laid out to receive regular watering in some parts, moderate watering (or rainfall alone) in other spots, be sure you don't mix plants with different water needs or tolerances. Those that need regular watering will suffer in the dry areas (if they live at all); the drought-tolerant types may languish and die with a steady moisture supply they don't need.

Design considerations

After you've narrowed the field of plant choices to those that will do well on your property, consider how they'll look in the landscape. Are the sizes and shapes pleasing? Will plants grouped together enhance each other? What sort of grooming will be required?

Compatibility. The majority of the plants we recommend are "good neighbors": their root systems won't seriously compete with adjacent plants for water and nutrients. A few choices, though, are shallow-rooted or somewhat competitive (*Acacia*, for example); several others have easily injured roots. For these, we suggest specific garden placements to avoid any compatibility problems.

Design harmony. Visualize the combined appearance of the plants in your garden. Consider the

colors and textures of foliage, the colors of flowers and their blooming times, and contrasting plant shapes. Careful planning here will help you avoid unsettling color clashes, the monotony created by uniform leaf colors or textures, or a jumbled appearance resulting from a haphazard assortment of plant shapes and sizes.

Size. Make your choices with a mind's-eye view of the garden at maturity. Before setting any plants in the ground, double-check their ultimate sizes and shapes. Extra care at this point can save you from repeated pruning (or even removal) of inappropriate choices in later years.

Be sure you know the growth rates of your plants. If you decide you don't want to wait 10 years for a tree to begin providing shade, pick another that will grow faster—or plant other fast-growing plants nearby for short-term effect.

Grooming. One way to cut down on maintenance time is to select plants that need little or no routine cleanup, grooming, or pruning in order to stay attractive. The plants described on pages 22 to 78 generally meet these easy-care criteria. We've screened out most plants that shed quantities of litter over long periods or that create messes from fallen fruits or spent flowers; for the few exceptions, we suggest particular garden placements to offset the problem. We have also eliminated a number of easy-to-grow plants that require dead-heading after flowering or routine pruning in order to produce the next year's blossom crop. Absent, too, are plants that need frequent dividing to remain attractive and in good health.

Personal satisfaction. When you have selected your easy-care plants, give your choices one last, critical review. Do you like their appearance and characteristics? Are you happy with their function in your garden? In the final analysis, your garden must have more than easy-care virtues—it must feature plants you find pleasing.

Maintenance Review

You've designed your garden, selected all structural materials, and chosen the perfect plants. Now it's time for one last, thorough review—your final chance to make sure that the garden you have devised is truly easy-care.

Check your plans against the listing of typical high-care features on page 6. If your garden passes the test, set up a maintenance calendar (see page 94). You'll find that regular maintenance done on schedule will be better for your garden—and easier on you.

Elegant entry path features just a few compatible plants, carefully chosen to remain in bounds without severe restriction. Maintenace is limited to grooming and watering. Landscape architects: Jeffrey W. Stone and Lois Sherr.

Wood, gravel, and green foliage *are the only elements in this peaceful, naturalistic service-entry planting. Creeping lily turf (Liriope spicata), shrubs, and trees are maintained on drip irrigation; herbicide keeps the pathway neat. Landscape design: Page Sanders.*

Flowing lawn, *kept in place by header boards, unites plantings of colorful lily-of-the-Nile (Agapanthus orientalis). Irregularly shaped paving stones are slightly recessed; the lawn spills over their edges, eliminating the need for frequent trimming. Landscape design: Robert Duranleau.*

Handsome Trees
Accent the Landscape

A tree is often the focal point of a landscape, the central element around which the rest of the garden is arranged. For this reason—and because removing an unsatisfactory tree can be a major project—it pays to choose your trees wisely. While many trees will grow easily, not all of them are good subjects for easy-care gardens; those recommended on the following pages meet the criteria outlined on pages 17 to 20. Many well-known and popular trees are included here, as well as some less familiar species that are sure to become favorites as their reputations spread. Missing from our selection are a number of frequently planted trees—eucalyptus and the large maples, for example—which, though attractive, fail to meet easy-care standards.

Even easy-care trees require some periodic attention. Though they demand no routine pruning, they may need (as noted) guidance when young to achieve a shapely form, or staking or early training to develop strong, upright trunks—care you'll have to provide for only a few years.

Every tree sheds leaves or needles—deciduous trees generally in autumn, evergreens often in spring—so you may need to clean up this litter every now and then. Many of our easy-care choices produce litter that quickly disintegrates or filters into plantings; in the few cases where litter may be a nuisance in certain circumstances, we give landscaping suggestions to minimize the problem.

Numerous easy-care trees provide color and shade. Magnolia soulangiana *(top left) enlivens the late winter/early spring scene, while crape myrtle* (Lagerstroemia indica, *bottom left) shines in summer. Graceful* Melaleuca quinquenervia *(right) offers decorative white bark all year.*

Acer palmatum

ACER

M A P L E

Pictured above

Zones: Vary
Growth rate: Moderate, to various heights
Soil: Needs well-drained soil
Water: Needs regular watering (except *A. circinatum*, *A. ginnala*)
Exposure: Varies

To millions of people, the maple is a well-known, if not a sentimental, favorite. Unfortunately, the big maples can't be considered good trees for easy-care gardens—but a number of smaller types fit comfortably into an easy-care scheme. The best known of these is the Japanese maple, *A. palmatum* (Zones 6–9 West, 5–8 East), a round-topped, spreading, single- or multitrunked tree growing to about 20 feet high and wide. It typically branches low to the ground, carrying foliage in horizontal layers. The five- to nine-lobed leaves are 2 to 4 inches long; new growth may be pink or red,

maturing to a bright, fresh green, then turning to red or yellow in autumn. The overall effect is airy, graceful, and delicate.

Numerous named selections are sold; those with red or red-purple foliage are the most common. Not all red-leafed trees retain their red color throughout summer; for color stability, look for 'Atropurpureum' or 'Bloodgood'. Keep in mind that many named varieties (especially those with deeply cut leaf margins) are slow-growing and shrubby.

Japanese maple thrives in full sun where there is atmospheric moisture: on the Atlantic seaboard, in much of the Pacific Northwest, and in coastal northern California. In areas where summer weather is hot and dry, trees need shelter from wind and a location that's partly shaded, especially during the hottest part of the day.

A favorite in its native Pacific Northwest is the vine maple, *A. circinatum* (Zones 5–9 West, 5–8 East). Grown in full shade, it may be crooked or sprawling—almost vinelike—but in partial shade or in the open, it's a multitrunked tree with a slightly irregular shape, reaching a height of 35 feet with vari-

able spread. Light green, five- to 11-lobed leaves are basically circular, to 6 inches across; autumn color may be yellow, orange, or red. Where summers are hot and dry, plant the tree where it will receive shade during the warmest part of the day.

Amur maple, *A. ginnala* (Zones 3–8), is an attractive, rugged tree, well suited to cold, windswept regions. For a 20-foot upright to spreading tree, train it to a single trunk; for a shrubbier effect, let several trunks develop. Leaves are up to 3 inches long, with three lobes; autumn color is brilliant red. Unlike other maples, Amur maple grows well in poor, dry soils.

Amur maple and vine maple will tolerate drought when established, but Japanese maple needs well-drained soil and regular moisture throughout the growing season. All three species tend to have shallow roots, so plant them in association with permanent shrubs and ground covers, and avoid digging the soil around the trees.

CELTIS

H A C K B E R R Y

Zones: Vary
Growth rate: Moderate, to various heights
Soil: Not particular
Water: Needs regular watering when young; established trees are drought-tolerant
Exposure: Sun

The hackberries look like scaled-down versions of some elms (to which they are related), but unlike elms, they're deep-rooted, so you can easily grow other plants beneath and close by. All have yellow autumn color and corky, ridged bark when mature. Small, berry-like fruits, appealing to birds, appear in summer and last into autumn. When established, hackberries will tolerate a variety of trying conditions: desert heat, strong winds, and dry, alkaline soil.

The largest species are Mississippi hackberry, *C. laevigata* (Zones 6–9), and common hackberry, *C. occidentalis* (Zones 3–10 West, 3–8 East). Each reaches 100 feet or more in the wild, though 50 feet is a more typical garden height.

Mississippi hackberry has a broad, rounded, fairly open crown; outer branches droop slightly. Common hackberry is irregular to rounded in form, about as wide as it is high, sometimes with pendulous branches. In its native territory (a large area extending from the Rocky Mountains to the Atlantic), common hackberry is subject to witches' broom disease. This condition isn't weakening, but it's not attractive— afflicted trees produce clusters of small twigs at branch ends. Chinese hackberry, *C. sinensis* (Zones 8–9), looks like a smaller common hackberry with glossier foliage; it's resistant to witches' broom disease. All three of these species leaf out in midspring.

European hackberry, *C. australis* (Zones 7–9), reaches 40 to 70 feet; it has a narrower crown and more upright branching than the other species, and remains leafless for a shorter period.

CERCIDIPHYLLUM JAPONICUM

K A T S U R A   T R E E

Zones: 4–9 (West), 4–8 (East)
Growth rate: Slow to moderate, to 50 feet
Soil: Needs well-drained soil
Water: Needs regular watering
Exposure: Sun; partial shade in hot-summer regions

Native to Japan, the Katsura tree is an elegant landscape asset. Tiny flowers bloom before leaves emerge in spring, forming a red-purple haze around the branches; leaves are nearly round, 2 to 4 inches across, with heart-shaped bases. New growth is bronze, maturing to dark blue-green (often grayish beneath), then turning brilliant yellow or red in autumn.

Trained to a single trunk, Katsura tree will grow narrowly upright for many years before starting to spread. But if several trunks are allowed to develop (and if lower branches are left in place), the tree takes on a broader shape— spreading to 50 feet, with branches angling upward and outward, carrying foliage in horizontal tiers. Katsura tree needs summer humidity and protection from scorching sun and drying wind.

CERCIDIUM

P A L O   V E R D E

Pictured at right

Zones: 8 and 9
Growth rate: Fast, to various heights
Soil: Not particular
Water: Not particular
Exposure: Sun

These trees are desert denizens, offering filtered shade and demanding no special care in return. The largest is blue palo verde, *C. floridum* (sometimes sold as *C. torreyanum*); with regular watering, it rapidly reaches a height and width of about 25 feet. An intricate mass of spiny, blue-green branches, twigs, and leaf stalks offers light shade (tiny leaflets, emerging in early spring, last only a short time). In spring, the entire tree is covered with short clusters of bright yellow blossoms.

Little-leaf palo verde, *C. microphyllum*, is generally similar to blue palo verde, but it's somewhat smaller. Bark and branches are yellowish-green; flowers are pale yellow. Sonoran palo verde (*C. praecox*), an umbrella-shaped tree growing up to 15 feet tall, has lime-green bark.

Though these amenable trees will survive if entirely neglected, they all improve in appearance with at least occasional watering—and will accept routine garden watering and fertilizing. They are best planted where litter from seed capsules can filter into permanent plantings.

Autumn Foliage Color

All are deciduous

Acer
Yellow, orange, or red

Celtis
Yellow

Cercidiphyllum japonicum
Yellow or red

Cercis canadensis
Yellow

Cornus
Glowing red or yellow

Fraxinus
Yellow or purplish

Ginkgo biloba
Stunning bright yellow

Lagerstroemia indica
Yellow, orange, or glowing red

Liquidambar styraciflua
Yellow, orange, pink, red, or purple

Pistacia chinensis
Luminous gold, orange, or red

Prunus
Yellow or red

Pyrus calleryana
Vibrant red shades

Quercus
Yellow, orange, red, or ruddy brown

Tilia cordata
Yellow

Zelkova serrata
Yellow, gold, or red

Cercidium

CERCIS CANADENSIS

E A S T E R N   R E D B U D

Zones: 5–9 (West), 4–8 (East)
Growth rate: Moderately rapid, to 35 feet
Soil: Needs well-drained soil
Water: Needs regular watering
Exposure: Sun to partial shade

Before its leaves emerge, the redbud treats you to an impressive display of small, sweet pea–shaped, rose-pink flowers that literally cover the tree, appearing on twigs, branches, main limbs, even the trunk. Blossoms later develop into flat, pea pod–like seed pods that look decorative during the winter months. Leaves are broad ovals with pointed tips, 3 to 6 inches long, turning yellow in autumn.

Redbuds grow fairly rapidly, forming slightly irregular, round-topped trees 25 to 35 feet tall; older trees carry their branches in horizontal tiers. Of the several selected varieties sold, 'Alba' (or 'White Texas') has white flowers; 'Rubye Atkinson' has blossoms of pure pink,

while 'Plena' (also sold as 'Flame') bears pink double flowers resembling rosebuds. Flowers of 'Oklahoma' are wine-red; 'Forest Pansy' has pink blossoms and purple foliage on reddish branches.

CORNUS

D O G W O O D

Zones: Vary
Growth rate: Moderate, to various heights
Soil: Needs good, well-drained, slightly acid soil
Water: Needs regular watering
Exposure: Sun; partial shade in hot-summer regions

The most widely planted—and widely adaptable—dogwood is the Eastern or flowering dogwood (C. *florida*, Zones 5–9), a good-looking tree at all times of year. At maturity, it's 25 to 30 feet tall and nearly as broad; branches spread horizontally with tips upturned. Flowers cover the tree in spring before leaf-out; each showy flower is up to 4 inches

across, consisting of four notched, petal-like bracts in white or pink. Leaves are oval, up to 6 inches long—bright green in spring and summer, brilliant red in autumn. A number of superior named forms are sold, including 'Pendula', with drooping branches, and several types with variegated foliage. 'Cloud Nine' performs well in a wide range of climates, both in the coldest regions of adaptability and where winter chill is slight.

Two other species—both naturally shrubby—are easily trained into small trees to about 20 feet tall. C. *kousa* (Zones 6–9), the Kousa or Japanese dogwood, can be grown with one trunk or several; branches are horizontal, wide-spreading (to about 20 feet), and densely covered with lustrous oval leaves that turn red or yellow in autumn. Japanese dogwood flowers after its leaves are out (about 3 weeks later than Eastern dogwood), bearing creamy white blooms to 2 inches long on upper sides of branches. In autumn, strawberrylike fruits hang beneath the branches.

Pagoda dogwood, C. *alternifolia* (Zones 5–9), is multitrunked and horizontally branching, about as tall as C. *kousa* but not as wide. Its small, creamy white flowers aren't as showy as those of other dogwoods, but autumn foliage display is just as fine.

Flowering Trees

(D) Deciduous; (E) Evergreen

Acacia baileyana (E)
Fluffy bright yellow blooms in winter

Callistemon (E)
Brushlike red, white, or yellow flowers

Cercidium (D)
Springtime display of yellow

Cercis canadensis (D)
Bright rose-pink in spring

Cornus florida, C. kousa (D)
White or pink blossoms in spring

Koelreuteria paniculata (D)
Yellow summer flowers

Lagerstroemia indica (D)
Bright or pastel summer flowers

Magnolia acuminata cordata (D)
Yellowish blossoms at leaf-out

Magnolia loebneri (D)
White or pink flowers

Magnolia soulangiana (D)
Impressive, large white to purple blossoms before leaves

Magnolia virginiana (D)
Fragrant white blooms all summer

Melaleuca (E)
Fluffy clusters in pastel shades

Pittosporum rhombifolium (E)
White spring flowers

Prosopis glandulosa torreyana (D)
Greenish flowers in spring, summer

Prunus (D)
Lavish spring display of pink or white

Pyrus calleryana (D)
Small white flowers in early spring

ELAEAGNUS ANGUSTIFOLIA

R U S S I A N   O L I V E

Zones: 3–9
Growth rate: Fast, to 25 feet
Soil: Needs well-drained soil
Water: Not particular
Exposure: Sun

Russian olive is a good-looking choice for a specimen tree, windbreak, or barrier planting. One of its special virtues is its ability to thrive in trying climates—through hot summers, cold winters, drought, poor soil, and wind. (Performance is poor, though, where summers are humid.)

Narrow, willowlike, silvery gray leaves to 2 inches long contrast effectively with the dark brown, shredding bark. Growth is upright and angular, to 20 to 25 feet, with equal spread.

The tree may have one or several trunks; trunk and branches may be armed with spines, but some nurseries offer thornless selections. Fragrant, silvery yellow summer flowers aren't too striking, but the fruits that follow are somewhat showier, resembling small, yellowish olives.

FRAXINUS

A S H

Zones: Vary
Growth rate: Fast, to various heights
Soil: Not particular; prefers deep soil
Water: Needs regular watering when young; established trees are somewhat drought-tolerant
Exposure: Sun

The ashes are generally tough, often thriving in situations that can defeat many other shade trees. Though most are medium to large trees, their foliage canopies appear almost delicate, since each leaf consists of numerous fairly small, narrow leaflets. Autumn color is usually yellow, sometimes purple; fallen foliage dries and crumbles quickly. In many species, male and female flowers are borne on separate trees; where the two grow nearby, female trees produce quantities of seeds, resulting in countless seedlings. For this reason, horticulturists have propagated male selections of the most useful species.

White ash, *F. americana* (Zones 4–9), is one of the tallest species, ultimately reaching 80 feet with a 40- to 50-foot spread. Variety 'Rosehill' is seedless, more pyramidal than oval in outline; autumn color is red.

European ash, *F. excelsior* (Zones 4–10 West, 4–9 East), is about the same size as white ash, but it doesn't change color in autumn. 'Kimberly' is a seedless selection especially suitable for the colder zones; 'Rancho Roundhead' grows 25 to 30 feet high and wide.

Variety 'Moraine' of *F. holotricha* (Zones 6–10) reaches a height of 35 to 40 feet, providing filtered shade beneath an upright, rounded canopy. Raywood ash, *F. oxycarpa* 'Raywood' (Zones 6–10), forms a rounded crown to 35 feet tall; leaves turn red-purple in autumn.

Green or red ash, *F. pennsylvanica* (Zones 3–8), is available in two superior seedless forms and one worthy hybrid. 'Marshall' (also sold as 'Marshall's Seedless') grows at a moderate rate to 40 to 60 feet tall and about half as wide; glossy, dark green leaves are fairly large. 'Summit' grows rapidly to about the same size. The hybrid 'Fan West' has light olive-green foliage; it's especially good for desert conditions, since it tolerates both drought and alkaline soil.

Widely available Modesto ash, *F. velutina* 'Modesto' (Zones 8–10), is too susceptible to diseases and pests to be recommended for easy-care situations. A much better selection, particularly for the alkaline soil of desert regions, is *F. v.* 'Rio Grande', the Fan-Tex ash. Its

Ginkgo biloba

large, dark green leaves emerge early in spring and last late into autumn before turning yellow. The mature tree is about 50 feet high and 30 feet wide.

GINKGO BILOBA

M A I D E N H A I R   T R E E

Pictured above

Zones: 5–10 (West), 5–9 (East)
Growth rate: Varies, to 50–70 feet
Soil: Needs well-drained soil
Water: Needs regular watering until established
Exposure: Sun

Though related to needle-leafed conifers, the graceful ginkgo looks like a broad-leafed deciduous tree. Each leathery, 1- to 4-inch-wide leaf is shaped like an open paper fan, wavy across the top with a cleft in the center. Leaves appear in late spring, remain a bright, rather light green until autumn, then suddenly turn to pure, bright yellow. A week or more after the color change, leaves drop—almost all at once.

Male and female flowers are carried on separate trees; females bear edible nuts encased in fleshy, foul-smelling coverings. For this reason, it's best to plant only male trees.

Though ginkgos generally grow upright, form ranges from fairly narrow to

spreading. For predictable configuration, try the named male selections 'Autumn Gold' (upright, eventually quite broad) and 'Fairmount' (pyramid-shaped).

Ginkgos grow slowly to fairly rapidly, depending on culture. For fastest growth, water and fertilize trees regularly when young; continue routine watering during dry periods until trees reach 15 to 20 feet. By then, the roots should be sufficiently established to get by with little or no supplemental water.

KOELREUTERIA PANICULATA

G O L D E N R A I N   T R E E

Zones: 5–9 (West), 5–8 (East)
Growth rate: Slow to moderate, to 35 feet
Soil: Not particular
Water: Needs regular watering when young; established trees are drought-tolerant
Exposure: Sun

Growing up to 35 feet high and wide, this tree casts filtered shade and thrives in some of the warmest climates where shade is most welcome. To maintain a symmetrical shape, young trees may need occasional corrective pruning.

Goldenrain tree begins its display in spring, when bright salmon-red new leaves emerge; each leaf is up to 15

. . . Koelreuteria paniculata

inches long, with seven to 15 oval, 3-inch leaflets. In midsummer, branch tips are decked out in 8- to 14-inch-long clusters of yellow flowers, followed by fruits that resemble paper lanterns—red at first, aging to buff and brown. Fruit lasts into winter; foliage drops in early autumn without assuming colorful tints.

LAGERSTROEMIA INDICA

CRAPE MYRTLE

Pictured on page 22 and at right

Zones: 7–10
Growth rate: Moderate, to 30 feet
Soil: Not particular
Water: Needs moderate deep watering when young; established trees are drought-tolerant
Exposure: Sun

Crape myrtle is one of the special glories of summer. Individual blossoms are small and crinkled, packed into foot-long clusters at branch ends; colors range from lavender, purple, and white to vivid shades of red, rose, pink, and orchid. Bark is especially attractive—smooth gray to light brown, flaking off to reveal patches of pink inner bark. Spring growth emerges bronzy green, then matures to oval, 1- to 2-inch leaves of glossy deep green; autumn color may be yellow, orange, or brilliant scarlet.

Crape myrtle can be grown as a single- or multitrunked tree or as a large shrub (see page 40). In recent years, more and more named selections have become available.

Expect good bloom from this plant only where summers are warm to hot. Mildew is a common problem in marginally warm areas; for these regions, the best choice is one of the mildew-resistant Indian Tribes named selections. Though crape myrtle is not particular about soils, its leaves may become chlorotic where soil is alkaline.

LIQUIDAMBAR STYRACIFLUA

LIQUIDAMBAR

SWEET GUM

Zones: 6–10 (West), 6–9 (East)
Growth rate: Moderate to fast, to 60 feet
Soil: Not particular; tolerates poorly drained soil
Water: Needs regular watering
Exposure: Sun to partial shade

Lagerstroemia indica

Liquidambar—or sweet gum, as it's known in its native eastern United States—grows straight and tall. Young and middle-aged trees are narrow to pyramidal; only in older specimens does the branch span broaden to about two-thirds the tree's height. Large, five-lobed leaves look much like the foliage of some maples. Flowers are quite inconspicuous, but the resulting seed vessels are striking: 1- to 1¼-inch balls covered with small sharp points, resembling tiny medieval maces. Many young twigs and branches have protruding, corky ridges of bark tissue. Brilliant autumn color varies from tree to tree (and sometimes from one year to the next); for a consistent display, choose one of the named selections. 'Burgundy' features dark, wine-purple leaves lasting well into winter; 'Festival' turns to shades of yellow, orange, and pink; 'Palo Alto' becomes brilliant orange and red.

Sweet gum's surface roots and hard seed vessels can be a problem in lawns and cultivated planting beds, so use the trees in the garden background (they're especially attractive in grove plantings) or where they can be underplanted with permanent shrubs or ground covers.

MAGNOLIA

Pictured on page 22 and on facing page

Zones: Vary
Growth rate: Varies
Soil: Needs good, well-drained soil
Water: Needs regular watering
Exposure: Sun to partial shade

The deciduous magnolias range in size from slow-growing plants that function as large shrubs for a number of years to imposing trees to around 80 feet tall. All should be planted where their roots won't be injured by digging.

Cucumber tree, *M. acuminata* (Zones 5–10 West, 5–8 East), is a fast-growing, dense, pyramidal specimen reaching 60 to 80 feet high and about 30 feet wide. Pointed oval leaves—5 to 11 inches long, 6 inches across—turn pale yellow in autumn. Greenish-yellow, 3-inch-long, tulip-shaped flowers bloom in late spring but are rather lost in the leaves.

For a small garden, a better choice is yellow cucumber tree, *M. a. cordata*. It grows at a moderate rate to only half the size of *M. acuminata*, but its 4-inch yellowish blossoms are considerably showier, since they appear just as the leaves start to emerge.

The hybrid *M. loebneri* (Zones 5–10 West, 5–9 East) can serve as either a shrub or a tree; it grows slowly to a height of 15 to 30 feet, with a rather open branch structure. Oval leaves are 4 inches long; 4-inch-wide flowers, each with 12 to 18 slender petals, appear before leaves emerge. Several named selections are available, including 'Leonard Messel' (pink) and 'Merrill' (white).

Saucer magnolia, *M. soulangiana* (Zones 5–10), is another hybrid that can function as an ever-enlarging, multi-trunked shrub; growing at a slow to moderate rate, it eventually reaches 25 feet high and wide. Early spring flower display is a crowd-stopper: cup-shaped blossoms to 6 inches across cover the leafless branches. Nurseries offer a number of named selections in a range of colors—white through pink shades to wine-purple, as well as some bicolors. Late-blooming variety 'Lennei', with purple and white flowers, is a good choice where late frosts might damage earlier flowers.

Saucer magnolia's oval 6-inch leaves are light to medium green, fading to brown in autumn. Gray-barked limbs make an attractive winter silhouette.

The southern native sweet bay, *M. virginiana* (Zones 5–10), assumes different forms in different climates; deciduous and shrubby in colder regions, it's a nearly evergreen 50-foot tree where summers are long and winters mild. Growth is moderate to rapid. Oval leaves to 5 inches long are gray-green on upper surfaces, nearly white beneath. Fragrant, rounded, 3-inch white flowers bloom in summer, followed by cucumber-shaped seed vessels. A native of marshes and swamps, sweet bay will take (but doesn't demand) more than the average amount of water.

PISTACIA CHINENSIS

CHINESE PISTACHE

Zones: 6–10
Growth rate: Moderate, to 60 feet
Soil: Not particular; tolerates alkaline soil
Water: Prefers regular watering when young; established trees are drought-tolerant
Exposure: Sun

If you live in a desert climate, Chinese pistache is your one choice for autumn foliage display—in the brightest possible shades of gold, orange, scarlet, or wine-red. Each leaf consists of narrow, pointed leaflets to 4 inches long; new foliage emerges bright pink. Flowers are inconspicuous; if male and female trees are planted near each other, female trees will bear clusters of small red fruits that turn dark blue when ripe.

Young trees may grow somewhat lop-sidedly, but mature into well-balanced specimens, particularly if given some pruning. ('Keith Davey' is a selected male variety with a more regular growth habit.) Regular watering encourages rapid growth, though verticillium wilt can affect regularly watered trees in areas of the Deep South and Southwest.

PROSOPIS GLANDULOSA TORREYANA

MESQUITE

Zones: 7–9
Growth rate: Fast, to 30 feet
Soil: Not particular; tolerates alkaline soil
Water: Not particular
Exposure: Sun

Magnolia soulangiana

Desert dwellers know mesquite as a friend—not just for barbecues but also for welcome relief from summer sun. This wide-spreading tree—to 40 feet or more—filters sunlight through a thicket of stems, leaf stalks, and tiny bright green leaflets. Small greenish-yellow flowers appear in spring and summer, followed by flat, beanlike pods to 6 inches long. Mesquite is typically multi-trunked; planted in a row, trees will interlace to make a screen and windbreak.

Argentine mesquite, sold as *P. alba*, casts denser shade than *P. g. torreyana*, since a greater amount of its blue-green foliage is evergreen. Another evergreen is 'Reese Hybrid'.

Mesquite adapts to desert drought, alkaline soil, even routine lawn watering. It grows best in deep soil where roots can probe far for moisture; in shallow soils, it usually remains shrubby.

Fast-growing Trees

(D) Deciduous; (E) Evergreen

Acacia baileyana (E)	**Fraxinus (D)**
Callistemon (E)	**Magnolia acuminata (D)**
Cedrus deodara (E)	**Melaleuca (E)**
Cercidium (D)	**Prosopis glandulosa torreyana (D)**
Elaeagnus angustifolia (D)	**Quercus palustris, Q. rubra (D)**

PRUNUS

FLOWERING CHERRY

FLOWERING PLUM

Pictured on page 6

Zones: Vary
Growth rate: Moderate, to various heights
Soil: Varies
Water: Prefers regular watering; will tolerate some drought
Exposure: Sun

(Continued on next page)

. . . Prunus

To many, flowering cherries and plums are the very breath of spring. Fortunately, a number of these small to medium-size trees are suitable for the easy-care landscape, though none is successful in desert regions.

Flowering cherry. The best-known flowering cherry, with the greatest available number of named selections, is Japanese cherry, *P. serrulata* (Zones 5–9 West, 6–7 East). Most of its named varieties are small trees with long, slender leaves that emerge along with or just before the flower clusters. Autumn foliage is yellow to tawny yellow. Perhaps the most common is 'Kwanzan' ('Sekiyama'), which provides some of the annual display at the Tidal Basin in Washington, D.C. Branches grow stiffly upright at a narrow angle, giving the tree an inverted cone shape to about 30 feet high by 20 feet wide. Deep rose-pink flowers in hanging clusters appear with red new foliage.

Broad horizontal branching distinguishes both 'Shirotae' ('Mt. Fuji') and 'Shirofugen'; the former grows 20 feet tall and over 20 feet wide, while the latter reaches about 25 feet in both directions. 'Shirotae' is early-flowering, with single to semidouble white blossoms that fade to purplish pink; 'Shiro-

fugen' blooms late, bearing double pink flowers that fade to white.

'Ukon' offers greenish-yellow flowers along with bronzy new growth on an open-structured tree to 30 feet high and wide. 'Amanogawa' departs from the usual growth habit—it's columnar, up to 25 feet tall but only 8 feet across. Light pink, semidouble flowers appear in midseason. 'Beni Hoshi' ('Pink Star') has arching, spreading branches that form an umbrella-shaped crown 20 to 25 feet high and wide; flowers are vivid pink.

Yoshino flowering cherry, *P. yedoensis* (Zones 5–9 West, 6–7 East), is another prominent Tidal Basin cherry. It's a fairly flat-topped tree, 40 feet tall by 30 feet wide, with a graceful, open pattern of curving branches. Blush pink, fragrant, single blossoms appear early in the season. Widely planted is *P. y.* 'Akebono' ('Daybreak'), which grows to 25 feet high and wide and bears darker pink flowers.

Largest among the flowering cherries is Sargent cherry, *P. sargentii* (Zones 4–9). Mature height is 40 to 50 feet; upright to spreading branches form a dense, rounded crown not quite as wide as the tree is tall. Single blush pink flowers emerge in small clusters before the red new growth; small black cherries are mostly hidden by leaves in summer.

Autumn foliage is red. Variety 'Columnaris' is narrowly upright.

Flowering cherries must have well-drained soil, since root rot is likely in continually damp or poorly drained soils. Though they'll tolerate some drought, they turn in their best performance if watered regularly. Prune to remove badly placed branches or to guide shape.

Flowering plum. The best-known, most widely planted flowering plums are purple-leafed selections or hybrids of *P. cerasifera* (Zones 5–9), the cherry-plum or Myrobalan plum. For an easy-care garden, the top choices among these are varieties bearing few or no fruits to litter patios or walkways. 'Krauter Vesuvius', a small tree to 18 feet high by about 12 feet wide, displays light pink flowers in late winter or early spring; purple-black leaves emerge after the blossoms and remain dark throughout the summer. 'Newport' is a larger tree—to 25 feet high and 20 feet wide—with pink flowers followed by red-purple foliage. A hybrid, *P. blireiana*, reaches about the same size as 'Newport'; semidouble pink flowers are followed by red-purple leaves that change to bronzy green by midsummer.

Flowering plums are much like flowering cherries in their pruning needs and in their soil and watering preferences, though the plums are less particular about well-drained soils and are a bit more drought-tolerant.

PYRUS CALLERYANA

C A L L E R Y   P E A R

Zones: 5–9
Growth rate: Moderate, to 50 feet
Soil: Not particular; tolerates poorly drained soil
Water: Prefers regular watering when young; established trees need moderate watering
Exposure: Sun

From the basic species of Callery pear—small, thorny, and horizontally branching—growers have selected and named several highly desirable forms. Most widespread is *P. calleryana* 'Bradford', a thornless tree to 50 feet high with a spreading branch pattern to about 30 feet across. Clusters of white blossoms appear in early spring, followed by small fruits that are inedible to humans but favored by birds. Broadly oval leaves are dark, glossy green; autumn color is striking carmine red.

Varieties 'Aristocrat' and 'Redspire' grow faster than 'Bradford', to about the

---

Shade Trees

(D) Deciduous; (E) Evergreen

Cedrus deodara (E)
Enormous, shady, tiered pyramid

Celtis (D)
Moderate shade and spread

Cercidiphyllum japonicum (D)
Light to moderate shade

Fraxinus (D)
Graceful form, dense shade

Ginkgo biloba (D)
Moderate, filtered shade

Liquidambar styraciflua (D)
Good shade in grove plantings

Magnolia acuminata (D)
Dense, spreading pyramid

Maytenus boaria (E)
Moderate, willowlike shade

Pistacia chinensis (D)
Graceful, feathery canopy

Prosopis glandulosa torreyana (D)
Filtered shade for desert

Pyrus calleryana (D)
Fairly dense shade

Quercus (D & E)
Good, dense shade from all oaks

Tilia cordata (D)
Dense shade

Tsuga (E)
Graceful tree, dense shade

Zelkova serrata (D)
Wide-spreading branches, dense shade

same height; they're pyramidal in shape, with upward-sweeping branches. Autumn color is purplish red in 'Aristocrat', yellow to red in 'Redspire'. 'Capital' and 'Whitehouse' have a narrow columnar form. All varieties have high resistance to fireblight, a disease that plagues many other pears.

QUERCUS

O A K

Pictured at right

Zones: Vary
Growth rate: Varies
Soil: Needs well-drained, deep soil
Water: Needs regular watering
Exposure: Sun

In addition to their beauty, most oaks are valued for their autumn color and for the welcome shade they cast in summer. All are long-lived, with strong wood not easily damaged by storms.

Round-crowned scarlet oak, *Q. coccinea* (Zones 5–9), reaches 60 to 80 feet; growth is moderately rapid. Because this tree has deep roots and an open-branched canopy, it's possible to grow grass or light shade–tolerant plants beneath it. Shiny, deeply toothed and lobed leaves to 6 inches long turn from bright green to scarlet in autumn.

Similar to scarlet oak is Shumard oak, *Q. shumardii* (Zones 6–9), a native of the Midwest and South. It's a good performer in alkaline soils. Autumn color is red to yellow.

Shingle oak, *Q. imbricaria* (Zones 6–9), has very un-oaklike foliage: each leaf is a narrow, dark green oval to 6 inches long. Young trees are narrowly pyramidal, growing at a moderate rate to about 75 feet high and half as wide, with a round-topped outline. Because the lower branches remain vigorous for many years, you can plant shingle oak as a windbreak or use it as a clipped hedge. Emerging spring foliage is bright red; autumn color is rusty red.

Pin oak, *Q. palustris* (Zones 5–9), is notable for its growth habit: upper limbs angle upward, middle limbs spread horizontally, and lower limbs angle downward. If you remove the downward-pointing limbs, the branches immediately above them will gradually point downward—and the tree will regain the shape you tried to change. Pin oak grows rapidly to 50 to 80 feet high by 30 to 40 feet wide; young specimens are slender and pyramidal, but mature trees are rounded and somewhat open. Glossy leaves, deeply cut into pointed

Quercus phellos

lobes, turn yellow, red, and then rusty brown in autumn, and remain on the tree well into winter.

Willow oak, *Q. phellos* (Zones 6–9), derives its name from its narrow, willowlike leaves—foliage that gives it the most fine-textured appearance of these deciduous species. Also like the willow, it performs well in moist soils. Moderately rapid growth produces a tree much like pin oak in size and outline. Autumn color is light yellow.

Majestic red oak, *Q. rubra* (Zones 4–10, is a fast-growing, deep-rooted, open-branched tree that will reach 90 feet with a spread of about 50 feet; young trees are pyramidal in shape, while mature specimens are broadly rounded. Lawns and plants that tolerate light shade grow well beneath its canopy. Lobed leaves, up to 8 inches long by 5 inches wide, emerge bright red in spring; autumn tints are dark red, ruddy brown, or orange.

Tilia cordata

SOPHORA JAPONICA

J A P A N E S E   P A G O D A   T R E E

C H I N E S E   S C H O L A R   T R E E

Zones: 5–10 (West), 5–8 (East)
Growth rate: Slow to moderate, to 40 feet
Soil: Not particular
Water: Not particular
Exposure: Sun

Here's a tree with nearly everything going for it. Small, oval, dark green leaflets give the canopy a soft, ferny effect. Starting in middle or late summer, foot-long, upright clusters of yellowish blooms resembling ½-inch-long sweet peas appear at branch ends; the display lasts for several weeks. Leaves fall in autumn without changing color, then dry and disintegrate quickly, eliminating the need for cleanup. Young wood is smooth and dark gray-green, but older bark has a more rugged look.

When you plant *S. japonica*, keep in mind that blossoms may not appear until the tree is about 5 years old, and that fallen flowers will leave yellow stains on concrete. For a faster-growing, more upright tree that flowers at an earlier age, look for variety 'Regent'.

Though Japanese pagoda tree is not particular about soil or water, it grows more slowly in clay soils than in lighter soils receiving regular water.

TILIA CORDATA

L I T T L E - L E A F   L I N D E N

Pictured at left

Zones: 4–9 (but not Midwest)
Growth rate: Slow to moderate, to 50 feet
Soil: Needs good, well-drained soil
Water: Needs regular watering
Exposure: Sun

Little-leaf linden is a well-mannered, attractive, dense shade tree for garden or lawn planting. Its pyramidal crown eventually achieves a spread of 15 to 30 feet. Branches are clothed in irregularly heart-shaped leaves to 3 inches across—dark green on upper surfaces, pale beneath, creating a shimmering effect in breezes. In colder regions, leaves turn yellow in autumn. Pendant clusters of small, fragrant, creamy white flowers, attractive to bees, appear in early to midsummer. Selected varieties 'Green-spire' and 'Rancho' have a narrower, more conical shape than the typical specimens.

Aphids may occasionally be a problem; their secretions can leave a sticky residue beneath the tree's canopy.

ZELKOVA SERRATA

S A W L E A F   J A P A N E S E   Z E L K O V A

Zones: 6–9 (West), 6–8 (East)
Growth rate: Moderate to fast, to 60 feet
Soil: Not particular; tolerates alkaline soil
Water: Prefers moderate, deep watering when young; established trees are drought-tolerant
Exposure: Sun

The decline of majestic American elms has spotlighted sawleaf zelkova as a good substitute—similar in looks, but disease-free.

Leaves are 2- to 5-inch-long ovals with toothed edges; autumn color is yellow, tawny gold, or orange-red. The tree spreads to 60 feet, its many ascending branches arising from nearly the same point on a short, stout trunk with smooth gray bark. Form ranges from urn-shaped to broadly spreading; the selected variety 'Village Green' comes close to duplicating the American elm's unique vase shape.

Give young trees deep watering to encourage deep rooting; shallow roots will send up suckers if they are disturbed. You may need to thin branches of young trees, leaving only the strongest and most symmetrically placed and heading back any that are overlong.

Drought-tolerant Trees

(D) Deciduous; (E) Evergreen

Acacia baileyana (E)	**Koelreuteria paniculata (D)**
Acer ginnala (D)	**Lagerstroemia indica (D)**
Cedrus deodara (E)	**Melaleuca (E)**
Celtis (D)	**Pistacia chinensis (D)**
Cercidium (D)	**Prosopis glandulosa torreyana (D)**
Elaeagnus angustifolia (D)	**Quercus (E)**
Fraxinus (D)	**Sophora japonica (D)**
Ginkgo biloba (D)	**Zelkova serrata (D)**

ACACIA BAILEYANA

B A I L E Y   A C A C I A

Zones: 9 and 10
Growth rate: Fast, to 20–30 feet
Soil: Not particular
Water: Needs moderate, deep watering when young; established trees are drought-tolerant
Exposure: Sun

For several weeks each January, Bailey acacia lights up the landscape with its brilliant yellow blossoms. The flowers—small, fluffy balls of stamens grouped in clusters—are so profuse that the foliage is almost completely hidden. When the tree is not in bloom, the finely cut blue-gray to gray-green leaves form a soft-looking, rounded crown up to 20 to 30 feet wide. Variety 'Purpurea' has lavender to purple new growth that later fades to gray-blue.

Acacias can be grown as single- or multitrunked trees. For best success, plant a small tree (1-gallon size or smaller); you're less likely to get a root-bound specimen, and a small plant's trunk strengthens more quickly. Acacias have some surface roots and produce fine litter from flowers, seed pods, and foliage, so it's best to place them in the garden background or where shrubbery or a ground cover can absorb the litter.

CALLISTEMON

B O T T L E B R U S H

Pictured above right

Zones: 10 and warmest areas of 9
Growth rate: Fast, to 25 feet
Soil: Needs well-drained soil; tolerates alkaline soil
Water: Prefers regular watering; tolerates moderate watering
Exposure: Sun

Callistemon's common name, bottlebrush, accurately describes its flowers: long stamens clustered tightly together around the stems. Woody seed capsules appear after the flowers and remain on the branches for several years; new growth continues from the tops of flower clusters. Both species recommended here also can be grown as massive shrubs.

Lemon bottlebrush, *C. citrinus*, becomes a rather narrow, round-topped tree if trained to one trunk. Its linear, 3-inch leaves are copper-colored when young, maturing to bright green. This species blooms several times throughout

Callistemon citrinus

the year, producing bright red flowers in 6-inch brushes. For best plant and flower quality, choose varieties 'Improved' or 'Splendens'.

White bottlebrush, *C. salignus*, is also a dense, slender tree with linear leaves that are pink to copper when young. Three-inch clusters of cream to pale yellow blooms appear in spring.

CEDRUS DEODARA

D E O D A R   C E D A R

Pictured at right

Zones: 8–10 and warmest areas of 7
Growth rate: Fast, to 80 feet
Soil: Not particular
Water: Needs regular watering when young; established trees are drought-tolerant
Exposure: Sun

The deodar cedar adds graceful majesty to a large garden as a specimen or background tree. In smaller gardens, several grouped trees can contribute soft beauty as a hedge or screen if you're willing to prune them each year in late spring.

Deodar cedar grows rapidly, producing an increasingly broad pyramid to about 40 feet wide, but the effect is graceful at all times: the main limbs

Cedrus deodara

. . . Cedrus deodara

usually angle upward a bit, but branch tips—even the tree's leader—are drooping. Two-inch needles in green, gray-green, blue-green, or blue-gray grow in tufted clusters; pale new growth in spring contrasts with darker mature needles.

Nurseries generally offer seed-grown plants varying considerably in needle color and plant density. Of the few named selections sold, 'Aurea' has yellow new growth that becomes greenish during summer; 'Glauca' is blue-gray.

MAYTENUS BOARIA

M A Y T E N   T R E E

Pictured at right

Zones: 9 and 10
Growth rate: Slow to moderate, to 30–50 feet
Soil: Needs well-drained soil
Water: Prefers regular watering; established trees tolerate moderate to little watering
Exposure: Sun

The mayten tree gives you all the delicacy and charm of a weeping willow, but it lacks the willow's size and invasive roots. Long, drooping branchlets extend from the main limbs, bearing narrow, bright green leaves that sway in the slightest breeze. Variety 'Green Showers' has denser foliage and broader leaves than the typical seed-grown tree.

To ensure upright growth, young trees should be staked until the trunk thickens enough to support the crown. If you want a single-trunked tree, thin excess growth and remove shoots from the base and low on the trunk; for a multitrunked specimen, encourage one or more shoots from the base. Plant where roots will not be disturbed; tree can send up suckers if roots are cut.

MELALEUCA

Pictured on page 22

Zones: 9 and 10
Growth rate: Fast, to various heights
Soil: Needs well-drained soil (except *M. ericifolia*)
Water: Not particular (except *M. linariifolia*)
Exposure: Sun

The melaleucas closely resemble their near relative *Callistemon* (page 33). The flowers are bottlebrush-type clusters of long stamens; new growth proceeds

Maytenus boaria

from the tops of flower clusters, while faded flowers form woody seed capsules.

M. ericifolia has inch-long, needlelike leaves reminiscent of heather foliage—hence the tree's common name, heath melaleuca. Early spring brings 1-inch spikes of yellowish-white blossoms. This tree is inclined to produce several trunks, each growing up to 25 feet tall; the tan or gray bark is soft and fibrous. Heath melaleuca performs well even in alkaline and poorly drained soils.

Flaxleaf paperbark, *M. linariifolia*, will eventually reach 30 feet, but needs to be staked for several years until the trunk becomes self-supporting. Bright green or bluish-green 1¼-inch leaves are stiff and needlelike; bark is white and sheds in papery flakes. In summer, the umbrella-shaped canopy is dotted profusely with small, fluffy white flower spikes. *M. linariifolia* prefers moderate watering.

Pink melaleuca, *M. nesophila*, naturally grows in a picturesque, irregular pattern: gnarled, heavy branches sprawl at first, then grow upward in a twisted fashion. But by staking up just one trunk, you can easily achieve a tree to

20 feet high. Bark is thick and spongy; thick, gray-green, inch-long leaves are nearly round. Clusters of 1-inch flowers—bluish-pink fading to white—bloom off and on throughout the year.

Cajeput tree, *M. quinquenervia* (sometimes sold as *M. leucadendra*), can reach a height of 40 feet. Main limbs grow upright, while young branches droop; light brown to nearly white bark is thick and spongy. The leaves are narrow ovals to 4 inches long; pinkish-red and silky when new, they become pale green, stiff, and glossy at maturity. Flowers are borne in summer and autumn, in 2- to 3-inch spikes; the usual color is yellowish-white, but you may occasionally see plants with pink or purple blooms.

M. styphelioides also grows up to 40 feet tall; its natural inclination is toward several trunks. Spongy bark darkens from light tan to charcoal with age. Branches are distinctly drooping, clothed in small, stiff, narrow, light green leaves. Creamy white blossoms in 1- to 2-inch clusters appear in summer and autumn.

PITTOSPORUM RHOMBIFOLIUM

QUEENSLAND PITTOSPORUM

Zones: 9 and 10
Growth rate: Slow to moderate, to 35 feet
Soil: Needs well-drained soil
Water: Prefers regular watering; tolerates moderate to little watering
Exposure: Sun to partial shade

Dark, glossy foliage, showy flowers, and colorful fruits make this evergreen tree especially handsome. The mature tree has a rounded crown and a somewhat open structure. Leaves are almost diamond-shaped, deep green with a highly polished finish. Clusters of small white flowers bloom in late spring, later forming hanging clusters of round $\frac{1}{2}$-inch fruits that turn yellow to orange in autumn. The fruits ripen through winter, then open to reveal sticky seeds and drop from the tree; fallen fruit can be messy on pavement. Aphids and scale may be occasional pests.

PODOCARPUS

Zones: Vary
Growth rate: Slow, to 60 feet
Soil: Needs well-drained soil
Water: Needs regular watering
Exposure: Sun; partial shade in hot, dry regions

These trees are botanically conifers, allied to pines, yews, arborvitaes, and the like. In appearance, though, the relationship is barely apparent. Instead of needles or scales, the various *Podocarpus* species bear $\frac{1}{4}$- to $\frac{1}{2}$-inch-wide leaves.

Fern pine, *P. gracilior* (Zones 9 and 10), has both juvenile and mature growth forms; plants sold as *P. elongatus* are simply the mature phase of *P. gracilior.* The juvenile form is upright, with glossy, dark green, 2- to 4-inch-long leaves widely spaced on branches. In the mature state, leaves are shorter (just 1 to 2 inches long), soft gray-green to blue-green in color, and spaced more closely on flexible branches.

Juvenile trees should be staked until the trunk becomes self-supporting. Young trees in the mature growth state (*P. elongatus*) have very limber trunks and branches, so they require more staking and training than do juvenile plants to assume a definite tree shape. Mature fern pines may eventually grow up to 60 feet tall and 30 feet wide.

Yew pine, *P. macrophyllus* (Zones 7–10), is stiffer and more upright in appearance than *P. elongatus,* with fairly horizontal main limbs and slightly drooping branchlets. Bright green leaves may reach 4 inches long by $\frac{1}{2}$ inch wide.

Both fern pine and yew pine may become chlorotic where soil is alkaline or poorly drained.

QUERCUS

OAK

Zones: Vary
Growth rate: Moderate, to 40–70 feet
Soil: Needs well-drained, deep soil
Water: Needs regular watering when young; established trees are drought-tolerant
Exposure: Sun

Though the choice among evergreen oaks is more limited than that among deciduous types (page 31), both *Q. ilex* and *Q. suber* make good all-year shade trees in the West and Southwest, growing to 40 to 70 feet high and wide.

Round-crowned holly oak, *Q. ilex* (Zones 7–10), has a dense canopy of oval 2- to 3-inch leaves—sometimes tooth-edged (like holly), sometimes smooth. Leaves are a rich, medium green on the top surface, yellowish or silvery beneath. Lower branches will remain healthy and continue to grow for many years, giving the tree the look of a mammoth shrub.

Like holly oak, *Q. suber* (Zones 8–10), the cork oak, is a round-topped tree with tooth-edged leaves that are dark above, pale beneath. It differs, though, in its thick, textured bark (used to produce commercial cork). The trunk and main limbs appear rugged and massive in contrast to the fine-textured foliage. Cork oak is a good shade tree in the desert, but may become chlorotic in alkaline soil.

TSUGA

HEMLOCK

Zones: Vary
Growth rate: Moderate, to various heights
Soil: Needs good soil (*T. caroliniana* needs acid soil)
Water: Needs regular watering
Exposure: Sun or partial shade

Gardeners in parts of the eastern United States value two native hemlocks for their delicate appearance and versatility. Both Canada hemlock (*T. canadensis,* Zones 5–9) and Carolina hemlock (*T. caroliniana,* Zones 5–7) can serve as exceptionally beautiful specimen trees or handsome, easily maintained hedges.

When mature, the Canada hemlock is a 60- to 90-foot, broadly pyramidal tree, often with two or more trunks. Branches are nearly horizontal, with drooping outer branchlets; dark green needles are arranged mostly in opposite rows. Carolina hemlock is a shorter, slimmer tree growing to about 40 feet high and 20 feet wide; its needles are arranged all around the branches rather than in opposite rows.

Both species are limited to climates featuring summer rainfall and humidity, and both require a location sheltered from strong winds. To maintain these trees as hedges of almost any height, trim or shear them in early spring.

Patio Trees

(D) Deciduous; (E) Evergreen

Acer circinatum (D)	**Lagerstroemia indica (D)**
Acer palmatum (D)	**Magnolia loebneri (D)**
Callistemon (E)	**Magnolia soulangiana (D)**
Cercidium (D)	**Melaleuca (E)**
Cercis canadensis (D)	**Podocarpus (E)**
Cornus (D)	**Prunus (D)**
Koelreuteria paniculata (D)	**Sophora japonica (D)**

Attractive Shrubs Unite House & Garden

Shrubs come in a multitude of sizes and perform a variety of garden functions. They often act as borders—directing traffic, lining walkways, and separating one area from another. But they can also unite structures with the landscape: the familiar foundation plantings create a smooth transition between house and yard, between indoor and outdoor living. Shrubs with attractive foliage provide a backdrop for plantings of annuals, perennials, and bulbs, then sustain the garden's visual appeal when flowers are not in bloom. Tall, dense shrubs function as green walls, screening views and creating a buffer between private yard and outside world. And then there are the spectacular flowering shrubs, treasured as beautiful garden accents.

Though easy-care shrubs serve the same functions as other shrubs, they require only minimal attention to remain attractive, healthy, and useful. The shrubs recommended on the following pages conform to the easy-care criteria outlined on pages 17 to 20. In addition, most of them need no routine pruning (assuming, of course, that you choose plants whose mature size suits your needs), nor do they require constant litter cleanup.

Subtle or showy? *Easy-care shrubs offer both choices. At left, bold red oleander* (Nerium oleander) *and feathery green juniper* (Juniperus) *stand out behind blue-flowered* Agapanthus orientalis. Pittosporum tobira *'Variegata' (top right) offers foliage in soft tones of gray-green and ivory. Striking color contrast makes the appropriately named* Hibiscus syriacus *'Red Heart' a showpiece.*

BERBERIS THUNBERGII

J A P A N E S E   B A R B E R R Y

Zones: 4–9
Growth rate: Moderate, to 6 feet
Soil: Not particular
Water: Needs moderate watering
Exposure: Sun to partial shade

Neat appearance and all-season interest make this a fine accent shrub, but its growth habit and density also recommend it for foundation, hedge, and low-barrier planting. Many slender stems arching in fountainlike fashion give the shrub a rounded appearance; small oval leaves are distributed in groups along the stems, a needlelike spine appearing beneath each grouping. Clusters of small, bright yellow flowers open in midspring, followed by ¼-inch red berries that blend with the brilliant autumn foliage at first, then last well into winter on bare stems.

The basic species has dark green leaves, but selections with colored foliage are widely planted. 'Atropurpurea' features bronze to purplish-red leaves that retain their color until autumn if planted in full sun. 'Ruby Glow' offers unusual variegated foliage in a marbled combination of creamy pink and bronzy red. 'Crimson Pygmy' is a dwarf version, about 2 feet high and spreading a bit wider; yellow-leafed 'Aurea' is about the same size. 'Kobold' is an all-green dwarf growing only about 1 foot tall.

CARAGANA ARBORESCENS

S I B E R I A N   P E A S H R U B

Zones: 2–8
Growth rate: Fast, to 20 feet
Soil: Needs well-drained soil
Water: Not particular
Exposure: Sun

Delicacy and indestructibility combine in this large shrub (or small tree, with training); it thrives even in semi-arid mountain and plains regions where strong winds, biting cold, and erratic to scant rainfall are the norm. Rounded, many-branched, and often spiny, it spreads about as wide as it is tall. Three-inch leaves consist of ½-inch leaflets in a fresh, bright green; fragrant yellow flowers shaped like sweet peas appear in small clusters along stems in late spring, well after leaves emerge.

Siberian peashrub makes a serviceable windbreak or barrier, its fine texture and clean color forming an attractive background to other plants.

CHAENOMELES

F L O W E R I N G   Q U I N C E

Pictured on facing page

Zones: 4–9
Growth rate: Moderate, to various heights
Soil: Not particular
Water: Needs moderate watering when young; established plants are somewhat drought-tolerant
Exposure: Sun

Plant flowering quince where you want a spectacular burst of color in late winter and early spring. Blossoming shrubs are arresting—2-inch flowers in white, pink shades, orange, or red cover the bare stems. Before leaf-out, the intricate, angular branch structure is attractive, and foliage is good-looking if not eye-catching: narrow 2- to 3-inch leaves are pink- to bronze-tinted when new, maturing to glossy green.

The nursery trade offers countless named hybrids, some growing upright to 6 feet or more, others with a lower, spreading habit. Most plants have spines; some varieties produce 3- to 4-inch fruits shaped like miniature quinces.

Because of its many thorny, interlacing branches, flowering quince makes a good barrier hedge and is especially attractive with a background of fence, wall, or evergreen hedge. Scale can be an occasional pest; plants may become chlorotic in alkaline soil.

CLETHRA ALNIFOLIA

S U M M E R S W E E T

S W E E T   P E P P E R B U S H

Zones: 3–9
Growth rate: Moderate, to 6–10 feet
Soil: Needs neutral to acid soil; tolerates poorly drained soil
Water: Needs regular watering
Exposure: Sun to partial shade

C. alnifolia's flowering season and fragrance are revealed in its common

---

Colorful Flowers & Fruits

(All are deciduous)

Berberis thunbergii
Flowers: yellow
Fruits: red

Caragana arborescens
Flowers: yellow

Chaenomeles
Flowers: white, pink, orange, red

Clethra alnifolia
Flowers: white, pink

Cotinus coggygria
Flowers: purple

Euonymus alata
Fruits: orange

Forsythia
Flowers: yellow

Hibiscus syriacus
Flowers: white, pink, red, purple shades

Lagerstroemia indica
Flowers: white, pink, red, lavender, purple

Ligustrum
Flowers: white
Fruits: blue-black

Lonicera
Flowers: white, yellow, pink
Fruits: red

Rhamnus frangula
Fruits: red to black

Viburnum
Flowers: white
Fruits: red

Chaenomeles

During spring and summer, winged euonymus is an attractive shrub with narrow, 2-inch leaves carried on horizontally spreading branches. But it's truly stunning in autumn, when it puts on the display that has earned it the common name "burning bush": the foliage turns a luminous pinkish-red, and the unusual pendant seed capsules (shaped like small hatboxes) split open, revealing orange seeds. After the leaves fall, the "wings"—corky ridges on either side of young twigs—become apparent.

Its dense, orderly growth makes winged euonymus a good choice for an unclipped hedge or barrier planting. A 10-foot-tall plant may spread up to 15 feet wide; for a smaller version, choose 'Compacta', which grows to only 4 to 6 feet high and wide.

FORSYTHIA

Zones: 5–9
Growth rate: Fast, to various heights
Soil: Needs well-drained soil
Water: Needs moderate watering
Exposure: Sun

Forsythias are among a handful of plants that give winter-weary gardeners an early signal that spring is just around the corner. While the rest of the landscape is bare and inactive, these shrubs explode into beacons of yellow as narrow-petalled blossoms cover the bare branches in late winter or early spring. During spring and summer, the pointed oval leaves create a neutral foil for other seasonal plantings.

Among the various species, named selections of *F. intermedia* offer the most spectacular and useful plants. 'Beatrix Farrand' grows in upright-arching fashion to 10 feet tall, bearing deep yellow flowers about 2 inches wide; 'Spectabilis' is a similar selection that's smaller-flowered and slightly shorter. 'Karl Sax' also resembles 'Beatrix Farrand', but it's lower and more spreading. Stiff, upright habit to 7 feet distinguishes 'Lynwood Gold'; 'Spring Glory' offers masses of yellow blooms on a 6- to 8-foot shrub.

All of the above varieties grow about as broad as they're tall and should be placed where they can comfortably reach their natural size, unrestricted by pruning. They make fine hedge or barrier plants where branches interlace, but because heading back sacrifices bloom, leave the sides of the shrubs unpruned. For best appearance and heaviest bloom, remove the oldest stems every year or two after the blooming season ends.

name, summersweet. For a month or more in middle to late summer, the upright stems are topped by 4- to 6-inch spikes of small white blossoms with prominent stamens. Two pink-flowered selections are 'Rosea', with pale pink flowers emerging from pink buds, and darker 'Pinkspire'. The oval, 4-inch leaves, thin-textured and prominently veined, turn from dark green to bright yellow or orange in autumn. Plants form clumps that enlarge slowly as new stems grow from the ground. Give summersweet partial or light shade where summers are hot; in cool-summer regions, it can take full sun and will thrive in gardens on the coast.

COTINUS COGGYGRIA

S M O K E T R E E

Zones: 5–10
Growth rate: Moderate, to 15–25 feet
Soil: Needs well-drained soil
Water: Needs moderate watering when young; established plants are drought-tolerant
Exposure: Sun

Smoke tree gets its name from the large, airy clusters of minute summer flowers that develop a smoky haze of purplish hairs as they fade. The basic species has

rounded, bluish-green leaves up to 3 inches long, but named varieties with purple foliage are more widely planted. 'Purpureus' gradually loses its purple color, becoming green during late summer; 'Royal Purple' remains a dark wine color until autumn. Both green- and purple-leafed types change color in autumn, turning to tawny gold, orange, or bright red.

Consider smoke tree for the background of a drought-tolerant garden, or for garden areas beyond the reach of regular watering—it actually *prefers* poor soil and little water. The shrub typically grows to 15 feet high and wide, producing several main branches from the ground, but you can achieve a treelike specimen about 25 feet tall by training it to a single trunk.

EUONYMUS ALATA

W I N G E D   E U O N Y M U S

B U R N I N G B U S H

Zones: 3–9
Growth rate: Slow to moderate, to 10 feet
Soil: Not particular
Water: Needs moderate watering
Exposure: Sun to partial shade

HIBISCUS SYRIACUS

R O S E   O F   S H A R O N

S H R U B   A L T H A E A

Pictured on page 37

Zones: 6–9
Growth rate: Fast, to 12 feet
Soil: Needs well-drained soil
Water: Needs regular to moderate watering
Exposure: Sun

In late summer, when garden color is often at a low ebb, rose of Sharon puts on a dazzling display of hollyhocklike blooms in white, red, pink shades, and purple hues from lavender to violet; some have reddish or purplish throats. The 2½- to 4-inch-wide blossoms may be single, semidouble, or double, depending on the variety. Most types with single flowers form seed capsules that aren't especially attractive; an exception is pure white 'Diana'.

Young rose of Sharon plants grow narrowly upright, gradually spreading to about half the plant's height. Coarse-textured, oval or lobed leaves emerge late, densely covering the plant, then drop in autumn without turning color.

Though these shrubs need no routine pruning, they may be grown as hedges and kept to a desired height. In Zones 6–8, apply a winter mulch to young plants for the first few years.

LAGERSTROEMIA INDICA

C R A P E   M Y R T L E

Zones: 7–10
Growth rate: Slow, to 4–8 feet
Soil: Not particular
Water: Needs moderate watering
Exposure: Sun

The flamboyant, frothy summer show of crape myrtle trees (page 28) can be enjoyed in shrub form as well. True dwarf and miniature plants offer the same flower color range and autumn foliage display as do the larger types, but on bushy plants normally growing no taller than 8 feet. The 'Petite' series, sold in named color selections, attain a height of 5 to 8 feet, with about the same width. Crape myrtlettes, usually sold as seeds, are smaller, ultimately reaching about 4 feet; you can expect blossoms 3 to 4 months after the seeds are sown in spring. Both sizes are excellent accent shrubs and striking hedge plants in warm-summer gardens.

Ligustrum 'Vicaryi'

Just like their larger cousins, these shrubby crape myrtles perform best where summers are warm to hot; mildew is a problem wherever climate is too cool or humid. Plants may become chlorotic in alkaline soils. Crape myrtle bears its flowers on new growth; you can limit size by heading the shrubs back lightly before spring leaf-out.

LIGUSTRUM

P R I V E T

Pictured above

Zones: Vary
Growth rate: Fast, to various heights
Soil: Not particular
Water: Prefers regular watering
Exposure: Sun to partial shade

Privets have a generations-old reputation as hedge plants, so it may be surprising to learn that they can also be good-looking individual shrubs. And if you think that "privet hedge" automatically means trimming, there's a further surprise in store for you: privets make attractive *untrimmed* hedges offering a late spring display of tiny white blossoms in lilaclike clusters. A crop of blue-black berries usually follows the flowers.

Amur privet, *L. amurense* (Zones 3–10), is the privet for cold-winter regions. Upright to somewhat spreading branches may reach 15 feet high; oval leaves are about 2 inches long, partially evergreen in mild-winter zones. Another variably deciduous privet, *L. ibolium* (Zones 4–10), is similar but has brighter green foliage; especially attrac-

tive is 'Variegata', its leaves edged in light yellow. For a striking pure yellow foliage plant, look for *L.* 'Vicaryi', Vicary golden privet (Zones 4–10). It's a rounded shrub growing to 4 feet tall.

LONICERA

H O N E Y S U C K L E

Zones: Vary
Growth rate: Moderate, to various heights
Soil: Needs well-drained soil
Water: Needs moderate watering
Exposure: Sun

The shrubby honeysuckles differ in detail but conform to a general pattern: upright to arching, twiggy but graceful; fragrant spring flowers with typical two-lobed honeysuckle shape; colorful fruits in summer or autumn.

The largest of the shrubby types is Amur honeysuckle, *L. maackii* (Zones 2–9), an upright-spreading plant to 15 feet tall. Late spring flowers are white, turning to yellow as they age, followed by berries that turn red in autumn; elongated, semiglossy leaves stay green until late in the year. *L. korolkowii* (Zones 6–9) is set apart from the other honeysuckles by its oval, blue-green to gray-green leaves. Pink flowers appear in late spring on an arching, spreading plant to 12 feet high; autumn fruits are red.

Tatarian honeysuckle, *L. tatarica* (Zones 3–9), features dark green foliage, pink flowers in late spring to early summer, and fruits that turn red by midsummer. It grows upright to 10 feet.

Nurseries offer several named selections with flowers in colors ranging from white to pink shades to nearly red.

An arching-spreading habit distinguishes Morrow honeysuckle, *L. morrowii* (Zones 5–9), which grows in mounding fashion to 6 feet high with greater spread. White flowers in late spring turn yellow as they age; red fruits ripen in summer.

The lowest-growing shrub honeysuckle is *L.* 'Clavey's Dwarf' (Zones 5–10), a rounded, 3-foot-tall plant densely outfitted in oval, bluish-green leaves. Small white flowers bloom in spring; they aren't very impressive, but the large red berries that follow in summer are showy.

The larger honeysuckle species are best used as accent plants and loose, graceful barrier or screen plantings; you can maintain all but Morrow honeysuckle as clipped hedges, but this sacrifices many flowers and fruits. Short 'Clavey's Dwarf' makes an excellent border or foundation planting.

RHAMNUS FRANGULA

A L D E R　　B U C K T H O R N

Zones: 3–8
Growth rate: Fast, to 15 feet
Soil: Not particular
Water: Needs moderate watering
Exposure: Sun to partial shade

One named selection has brought this plant to landscape prominence: 'Columnaris', the tall hedge buckthorn. Up-right, uniform, and densely foliaged, it's the perfect hedge for gardeners who don't want to bother with trimming. Though it can reach 15 feet high, its ultimate width is about 4 feet; to maintain as a hedge, simply limit it to whatever height suits you. Glossy, oval, dark green leaves to 3 inches long turn bright yellow in autumn. Insignificant flowers produce small, berrylike fruits that turn red, then black.

VIBURNUM

Pictured at right

Zones: Vary
Growth rate: Moderate, to various heights
Soil: Not particular
Water: Prefers regular watering
Exposure: Sun to partial shade

Mention *Viburnum*, and "snowball bush" comes to mind—largely because of the old favorite *V. opulus* 'Roseum' (common snowball), with its midspring display of spherical white flower clusters. Unfortunately, it's a special favorite of aphids, enough so that it doesn't qualify as easy-care. The species we recommend aren't entirely pest-free—they may be visited occasionally by aphids, spider mites, thrips, or scale—but they aren't likely to be overwhelmed.

Fragrant snowball, *V. carlcephalum* (Zones 5–9), grows upright to 10 feet tall by about 5 feet wide. Fragrant snowball clusters are 4 to 5 inches wide; semiglossy foliage is grayish-green. Chinese snowball, *V. macrocephalum macro-*

Viburnum plicatum plicatum

cephalum (Zones 6–9; totally deciduous only in Zones 6–7), is a large, rounded shrub, sometimes as tall as 20 feet, with correspondingly large (6- to 8-inch) "snowballs." Leaves are a lusterless dark green. Japanese snowball, *V. plicatum plicatum* (Zones 4–9), may reach 15 feet high and wide. Branches spread in horizontal tiers; snowball-like 3-inch flower clusters line both sides of the branches. Dark green leaves to 6 inches long turn purple in autumn.

Doublefile viburnum, *V. plicatum tomentosum* (Zones 4–9), is similar to Japanese snowball in growth habit and foliage, but it features flat flower clusters in "lace cap" formation: tiny fertile flowers in the cluster's center are surrounded by one or more rows of showy sterile blossoms. Variety 'Mariesii' has the showiest sterile flowers. Bright red, fruits ripen after the blossoms fade.

Another lace cap viburnum is the cranberry bush (*V. trilobum*, Zones 3–9); the common name derives from the red, edible fruits this shrub bears in autumn. Flower clusters to 4 inches across decorate a rounded plant to 15 feet high and wide; maplelike foliage turns brilliant red in autumn.

Neither lace cap nor snowball, densely foliaged linden viburnum (*V. dilatatum*, Zones 5–9) features 5-inch clusters of tiny ivory flowers followed by bright red fruits that ripen in early autumn and last well into winter. This shrub may reach 10 feet high and wide; nearly round gray-green leaves turn rusty red before dropping.

Autumn Color

(D) Deciduous; (E) Evergreen

■ **Abelia grandiflora (E)** Bronzy green	■ **Lagerstroemia indica (D)** Yellow, orange, red
■ **Berberis thunbergii (D)** Red	■ **Mahonia aquifolium (E)** Bronze-purple
■ **Clethra alnifolia (D)** Yellow, orange	■ **Nandina domestica (E)** Red
■ **Cotinus coggygria (D)** Gold, orange, red	■ **Rhamnus frangula (D)** Yellow
■ **Euonymus alata (D)** Pinkish-red	■ **Viburnum (D)** Red, purple

ABELIA GRANDIFLORA

G L O S S Y   A B E L I A

Pictured at right

Zones: 7–10; partially deciduous in Zones 7 and 8
Growth rate: Moderate, to 8 feet
Soil: Needs well-drained soil
Water: Needs regular watering
Exposure: Sun to partial shade

Though glossy abelia can't be described as showy, it's always graceful and attractive—and what the blossoms lack in flamboyance, they make up for in a summer-long display.

Arching stems form a rounded, fine-textured, fairly dense plant, growing up to 8 feet high and wide if unrestricted. Glossy oval leaves to 1½ inches long are bronzy when new, dark green when mature; in autumn and winter, they may take on bronze tints again. Small, trumpet-shaped flowers are scattered over the shrub in small clusters during summer. The usual blossom color is white, sometimes with a pink tint, but 'Edward Goucher'—the most popular of several named selections sold at nurseries—has orange-throated pink flowers on a plant to about 5 feet high. 'Sherwoodii', only 3 to 4 feet tall, bears white flowers on broadly spreading branches. 'Prostrata' is lower still—up to just 2 feet—and can be used as a ground cover.

A. grandiflora will be killed to the ground if the temperature falls to 0°F/ −18°C but will resprout to produce knee-high flowering shrubs by midsummer.

AUCUBA JAPONICA

J A P A N E S E   A U C U B A

Pictured at right

Zones: 7–10
Growth rate: Moderate, to 10–15 feet
Soil: Prefers well-drained soil
Water: Prefers regular watering when young; established plants are somewhat drought-tolerant
Exposure: Partial shade to shade

For the shaded garden, Japanese aucuba is an indispensible shrub. It thrives in dense shade, light shade, and filtered sunlight; it even prospers when competing with tree roots. But it's not a good choice for sunny spots—except in cool-summer regions, direct sun may cause sunburn and defoliation.

Abelia grandiflora **'Edward Goucher'**

Leathery, glossy leaves are oval in shape, up to 8 inches long; their size and density—and the plant's broad-as-tall proportions—give Japanese aucuba a bulky appearance. Dark red flowers are small and inconspicuous, but female plants bear showy red berries from autumn through winter if a male plant is nearby for pollination.

Numerous varieties have been selected for their attractive foliage. The most widely available are those with variegated leaves—yellow-centered, edged with yellow or cream, or yellow-spotted ('Variegata', the gold dust plant). For a smaller Japanese aucuba, choose all-green 'Nana'—it grows only 3 feet tall.

Mealybugs and spider mites may occasionally bother Japanese aucuba, especially if plants are in cramped quarters where air circulation is poor.

CALLISTEMON

B O T T L E B R U S H

Zones: 9 and 10 (West)
Growth rate: Fast, to various heights
Soil: Needs well-drained soil; tolerates saline and alkaline soils
Water: Prefers regular watering
Exposure: Sun

Lemon bottlebrush (*C. citrinus*) is the most widely planted bottlebrush species, and for good reason. It's pest-free, grows with no special care, and flowers on and off throughout the year. A large, rounded shrub (or tree—see page 33), it reaches 10 to 15 feet high; prominent stamens give the 6-inch red blossom spikes their brushlike look. Flowers are carried at branch tips; when they fade,

woody, somewhat decorative seed capsules are left behind. New growth proceeds from the ends of blossom spikes; the narrow 3-inch leaves are an attractive bright copper when they emerge.

For best flower and foliage quality, choose a named selection such as 'Improved' or 'Splendens'. 'Compacta' grows to about a third the size of the basic species; leaves and flower spikes are a bit smaller. Variety 'Jeffersii' offers a different flower color—red-purple aging to lavender—on a more rigid, 6-foot shrub. *Callistemon* 'Rosea' resembles a slightly taller *C. c.* 'Jeffersii', but blossoms are rose-pink.

Similar to *C. citrinus* is *C. phoeniceus,* the fiery bottlebrush. It is stiffer and more angular than lemon bottlebrush, and only about half as tall. Leaves are grayish-green; 4-inch red blossoms appear in both spring and autumn.

CAMELLIA

Zones: 8–10 (except desert)
Growth rate: Slow to moderate, to various heights
Soil: Needs well-drained, acid to neutral soil
Water: Prefers regular watering; established plants will tolerate moderate watering
Exposure: Shade to partial shade

To gardeners in the South and on the Pacific Coast, the camellia is a basic, trouble-free landscape shrub, valued both for its handsome, glossy foliage

Aucuba japonica

and the showy flowers it bears from late autumn through early spring.

The most widely grown camellias are varieties of *C. japonica*: upright (to 15 feet), spreading plants with thick, lustrous, broadly oval leaves and 3- to 6-inch, single to double blossoms in white, pink, red, and variegated combinations. Sasanqua camellias (varieties of *C. sasanqua*, *C. hiemalis*, and *C. vernalis*) are generally shorter, smaller-leafed, more willowy plants, with smaller flowers in early autumn through early winter. Grown to a lesser extent are reticulata camellias (varieties of *C. reticulata*)—tall, lanky plants with dull green foliage, noted for large, magnificent blossoms. Hybrid camellias—frequently crosses between *C. japonica* and lesser-known species—constitute a highly varied assortment of plant habits and flower sizes. Many were bred for adaptability to sun and low temperatures.

If you pay special attention to a camellia's needs at planting time and during its first few years, you'll find it an easy-care plant later on. First, choose a location sheltered from strong wind and protected from hot afternoon sun. Plant the shrub in well-drained soil amended with organic matter; set the plant so the top of the root ball is 2 to 3 inches higher than the surrounding soil level, then mulch thoroughly. Water regularly for several years to get the root system established; thereafter, the shrub needs only moderate watering. Scale and camellia petal blight are possible problems.

CISTUS

ROCKROSE

Zones: 8–10 (West), 8 (East)
Growth rate: Fast, to various heights
Soil: Not particular
Water: Prefers moderate watering; established plants are drought-tolerant
Exposure: Sun

Cheery rockroses nearly smother themselves in bloom during their late spring or summer flowering season; each flower lasts just one day, but a succession of buds carries display for 3 to 4 weeks. Blossoms resemble single roses with crepe paper–textured petals; foliage is lightly aromatic.

Rockroses can be pinched or lightly pruned for bushiness, but they generally look good if allowed to grow at will. They're happy directly at the coast or in the heat of the low desert, thriving with little or no water but accepting regular watering if soil is well drained. Use them in mixed beds of plants with low

water requirements, or mass them in areas receiving little attention.

White rockrose, *C. hybridus* (sometimes sold as *C. corbariensis*), a mounded plant 2 to 5 feet tall, has yellow-centered white flowers to 1½ inches across in spring. Crimson-spot rockrose (*C. ladanifer*) looks much the same, but the 3-inch white summer flowers have a dark red spot at each petal base. Pink-flowered, gray-foliaged *C.* 'Doris Hibberson' mounds to 3 feet high; 3-inch blossoms appear in early summer. Orchid rockrose, *C. purpureus*, also flowers in early summer; its 3-inch orchid-purple flowers have red-spotted petal bases. Vivid magenta, 2-inch flowers and roundish, furry leaves distinguish *C. incanus* (also sold as *C. creticus*), a dense, mounding plant 3 to 5 feet tall.

DODONAEA VISCOSA

HOP BUSH

HOPSEED BUSH

Zones: 9 and 10 (West)
Growth rate: Fast, to 12–15 feet
Soil: Not particular
Water: Not particular
Exposure: Sun

Undemanding hop bush is equally at home in seacoast and desert gardens, in well-watered landscapes and drought-tolerant schemes. Though it's a rounded plant about equal in height and width, its upright, branching habit and linear leaves give it a vertical appearance.

(Continued on next page)

Colorful Flowers & Fruits

(All are evergreen)

Abelia grandiflora
Flowers: white, pink

Aucuba japonica
Fruits: red

Callistemon
Flowers: red, red-purple, pink

Camellia
Flowers: white, pink, red

Cistus
Flowers: white, pink, purple

Elaeagnus
Fruits: red

Escallonia
Flowers: white, pink, red

Euonymus fortunei 'Carrieri'
Fruits: orange

Ilex
Fruits: red

Ligustrum japonicum
Flowers: white
Fruits: blue-black

Mahonia aquifolium
Flowers: yellow
Fruits: blue-black

Myrtus communis
Flowers: white
Fruits: blue-black

Nandina domestica
Flowers: white
Fruits: red

Nerium oleander
Flowers: white, yellow, pink, red

Osmanthus delavayi
Flowers: white

Pittosporum tobira
Flowers: white

Raphiolepis indica
Flowers: white, pink

Rhododendron
Flowers: white, pink, red, purple, yellow, cream

Taxus
Fruits: red

Viburnum
Flowers: white
Fruits: blue-green

. . . Dodonaea viscosa

Hop bush is strictly a foliage plant; though it does bloom, the flowers are virtually invisible. It's useful as a striking accent shrub, background screen planting, or unclipped hedge. The most popular variety is 'Purpurea', the purple hop bush. Narrow, 4-inch, bronzy wine leaves take on a deeper hue during winter. For truer purple foliage, look for burgundy-leafed 'Saratoga'. Both varieties need a sunny location to maintain leaf color; in shaded spots, foliage turns bronzy green.

ELAEAGNUS

Pictured below

Zones: 7–10
Growth rate: Fast, to various heights
Soil: Not particular
Water: Needs moderate watering when young; established plants are drought-tolerant
Exposure: Sun

The various *Elaeagnus* species are not showpiece shrubs, but they are ideal choices for barriers, screens, and high hedges—situations where their quiet beauty can serve as backdrop to more assertive plants. Silverberry, *E. pungens*, builds to a large, rounded shrub 8 to 15 feet high and wide (size is easily restricted by pruning). Tiny, rusty brown dots cover the spiny branches and wavy-edged, grayed olive green leaves. Inconspicuous but fragrant flowers appear in autumn, followed in spring by red berries with a silvery bloom. More widely available than the species are several somewhat lower-growing variegated selections: 'Variegata', with light yellow leaf margins; 'Marginata', with white-edged leaves; and 'Maculata', with gold-centered leaves rimmed in green. For larger, more silvery leaves, look for the variety 'Fruitlandii'.

Thornless branches growing upright to 12 feet distinguish *E. ebbingei* (sometimes sold as *E. macrophylla* 'Ebbingei'). New foliage is silver-tinted; mature leaves are dark green with silvery undersides. Like *E. pungens*, this shrub has fragrant flowers and red fruits—but it blooms in late spring, with fruits ripening in summer.

ESCALLONIA

Pictured at right

Zones: 9 and 10
Growth rate: Fast, to various heights
Soil: Needs well-drained soil; will not tolerate alkaline soil
Water: Prefers regular watering
Exposure: Sun to partial shade

Escallonias rank high among desirable barrier, hedge, and screen plants. The foliage is dense, neat, and glossy; plants need little shaping, and many types have a prolonged flowering period. Nurseries offer a number of species and varieties, all featuring small, bell-shaped blossoms carried in clusters at the ends of new growth.

Upright-growing *E. rubra* can reach a height of 15 feet if not headed back; red flowers appear throughout most of spring and summer. Variety 'C. F. Ball' resembles the species, but it's shorter—8 to 9 feet tall—and can be kept lower with periodic heading back and pinching.

E. exoniensis 'Balfouri', another fairly tall variety, reaches 10 feet; branches are drooping rather than upright. Summer flowers are white with a pink tinge. Variety 'Frades' (often sold under the name *E.* 'Fradesii') produces pink flowers during the most of the year on a compact 6-foot plant.

Among the *E. langleyensis* selections, 'Apple Blossom', a spreading plant to 5 feet high, is the most widely available. White-throated light pink flowers bloom from late spring through summer. For a still smaller plant (to 3 feet high), look

Escallonia langleyensis
'Apple Blossom'

for 'Compakta', with rose-red flowers.

These shrubs excel in seacoast gardens, but they also thrive in hot-summer regions if planted in partial shade.

EUONYMUS FORTUNEI

Zones: 5–9
Growth rate: Moderate, to various heights
Soil: Not particular
Water: Needs moderate watering
Exposure: Sun to shade

Though normally vining (page 54), *E. fortunei* also exists in a number of shrubby forms—all neat, undemanding plants, good-looking throughout the year. Cold-winter gardeners know them as one of the few broad-leafed evergreens that can survive subzero temperatures. Green-leafed varieties serve well as hedge, foundation, and mass plantings and as foils for more colorful plants; those with variegated foliage can also be used as accents. All have lustrous, leathery, oval leaves 1 to 2 inches long.

Elaeagnus pungens **'Maculata'**

Variety 'Carrieri', a green-foliaged type, is a spreading plant that can reach 6 feet tall; in autumn, it may bear showy orange fruits. 'Silver Queen' differs only in its white-margined leaves.

Other green-leafed selections—all with upright growth habit—include 'Sarcoxie' and 'Emerald Pride' (to about 4 feet tall) and 'Emerald Charm' (to about 6 feet). 'Golden Prince', eventually reaching a height of 4 to 5 feet, offers yellow-tipped new growth that matures to solid green.

For variegated selections, look for 'Emerald Gaiety' and 'Emerald 'n' Gold'. Both grow upright to 4 to 5 feet; the former has white-margined leaves, the latter yellow-edged foliage.

ILEX

HOLLY

Zones: Vary
Growth rate: Slow to moderate, to various heights
Soil: Needs good, well-drained soil
Water: Needs regular watering
Exposure: Sun to partial shade

The word "holly" immediately suggests red berries and spiny leaves, as typified by English holly (*I. aquifolium*). But not all hollies have red berries, many lack spiny foliage, and relatively few will set fruit without a male plant nearby for pollination. The following three hollies, however, are self-pollinating types bearing red berries.

Chinese holly, *I. cornuta* (Zones 7–10), is a mounded shrub up to 10 feet high and wide; its rectangular leaves carry a spine at each corner. Numerous named selections are sold, varying in leaf character and growth habit. Moderately fast-growing 'Burfordii', Burford holly, is the most widely available; it bears the characteristically large red berries, but its rounded leaves are typically spined only at the tip. Spiny-leafed selections include 'Dazzler' and 'Femina'; berry-producing dwarf varieties are 'Berries Jubilee' and 'Dwarf Burford'.

Much of English holly's character is retained in its hybrid *I. aquipernyi*, which bears heavy crops of red berries. Variety 'Brilliant', densely clothed in lightly spiny leaves, is a slow-growing, pyramidal plant reaching 10 feet or more.

Native American yaupon, *I. vomitoria* (Zones 7–10), differs in several respects from the previous two species. It is taller—almost treelike—reaching 15 to 20 feet; the dark green, inch-long leaves are spineless; and it tolerates alkaline soil. Berries are small but amazingly plentiful. Dwarf varieties are also sold.

JUNIPERUS

JUNIPER

Pictured on page 36

Zones: Vary
Growth rate: Moderate to fast, to various heights
Soil: Prefers well-drained soil
Water: Prefers moderate watering
Exposure: Sun

Juniper is the ubiquitous evergreen: wherever you live, there's likely to be at least one juniper available in the nearest garden center. Many varieties are sold in the nursery trade, ranging from ground-hugging mats to shrubs that can be broadly spreading, vase-shaped, arching, spherical, conical, or spirelike. Juvenile foliage consists of tiny, prickly needles, while adult foliage resembles overlapping scales. Some varieties are entirely juvenile, others entirely adult; still others have foliage of both phases. Color ranges from blue, gray, or olive through bright or dull green to purple-tinted or variegated with gold or cream. The following species are responsible for nearly all named varieties: *J. chinensis* (Zones 4–10), *J. communis* (Zones 2–9),

J. sabina (Zones 4–10), *J. squamata* (Zones 4–10), *J. scopulorum* (Zones 4–10), and *J. virginiana* (Zones 3–10). Consult a catalog or visit a well-stocked nursery to learn about available varieties.

Larger junipers are good screen, barrier, windbreak, or accent plantings; the lower, spreading shrubs often are massed as foundation plantings, low barriers, or high ground covers. These shrubs aren't particular about soil pH, but they won't succeed in continually moist soil. Possible pests include aphids, spider mites, twig borers, scale, and twig blight. In apple-growing areas, *J. virginiana* and its varieties are susceptible to cedar-apple rust.

LIGUSTRUM JAPONICUM

JAPANESE PRIVET

WAXLEAF PRIVET

Zones: 7–10
Growth rate: Fast, to 12 feet
Soil: Needs well-drained soil
Water: Prefers regular watering
Exposure: Sun to partial shade

(Continued on next page)

Hedges & Screens

(D) Deciduous; (E) Evergreen

Abelia grandiflora (E)	**Juniperus (E)**
Berberis thunbergii (D)	**Lagerstroemia indica (D)**
Callistemon citrinus (E)	**Ligustrum (D)**
Camellia japonica (E)	**Ligustrum japonicum (E)**
Caragana arborescens (D)	**Lonicera (D)**
Chaenomeles (D)	**Myrtus communis (E)**
Dodonaea viscosa (E)	**Nerium oleander (E)**
Elaeagnus (E)	**Osmanthus heterophyllus (E)**
Escallonia (E)	**Pittosporum tobira (E)**
Euonymus alata (D)	**Raphiolepis indica (E)**
Euonymus fortunei (E)	**Rhamnus frangula (D)**
Forsythia (D)	**Taxus (E)**
Hibiscus syriacus (D)	**Viburnum tinus (E)**
Ilex (E)	

Nandina domestica

. . . Ligustrum japonicum

This shrub radiates good health all year long. Each glossy, leathery-textured leaf is a 2- to 4-inch-long oval, dark green on the top, light green to nearly white beneath. Against this dense backdrop, the spikes of tiny white spring flowers stand out conspicuously. Some nurseries may sell *L. japonicum* as *L. texanum*—confusing, since there's another suitable easy-care variety, *L. j.* 'Texanum', which is a shorter (6- to 9-foot) variant of the species. Other varieties include 4- to 5-foot-tall 'Rotundifolium' (sometimes sold as 'Coriaceum'), with nearly round leaves, and 'Silver Star', its leaves attractively mottled with gray and edged in ivory.

MAHONIA AQUIFOLIUM

O R E G O N   G R A P E

Zones: 5–10 (West), 5–8 (East)
Growth rate: Moderate, to 7 feet
Soil: Not particular
Water: Needs moderate watering
Exposure: Sun to partial shade

Though "grape" accurately describes the appearance of *M. aquifolium*'s fruits, the strikingly handsome foliage suggests an alternate name: "Oregon holly." Each leaf consists of a long central leaf stalk with spiny-edged leaflets up to 3 inches long on either side. Light bronze when new, the glossy leaflets mature to medium green, then frequently turn bronze-purple during winter. Numerous stems rise from the ground, some upright, some spreading; they branch low

(or will branch low, with judicious heading back), forming an upright, rounded plant that's fairly well clothed with leaves. Bulk increases over the years as new stems rise from ground level and expand the clump's diameter. Clusters of small yellow flowers sit atop stems in early to midspring; these are followed by clusters of pea-size blue-black fruits dusted with a gray bloom. Variety 'Orange Flame' has brightly colored new growth and winter foliage.

Oregon grape will grow in full sun where summers are cool, but should be planted in partial shade in hot-summer regions. In such partial shade locations, and in cool-summer areas, plants tolerate considerable drought.

MYRTUS COMMUNIS

M Y R T L E

Zones: 9 and 10
Growth rate: Moderate, to various heights
Soil: Needs well-drained soil
Water: Needs moderate watering when young; established plants are drought-tolerant
Exposure: Sun to partial shade.

Throughout the year, myrtles are the picture of health. Narrow, glossy, aromatic 2-inch leaves with pointed tips densely cover upright stems; in summer, the dark green background is dotted with small white flowers, later followed by pea-size blue-black fruits. Myrtles naturally assume a rounded

form, growing to 6 feet or taller and just as wide, but you can trim, shear, or prune them to almost any size or shape.

Nurseries may offer a number of named selections, varying in foliage color and overall size. 'Buxifolia' has oval, boxwoodlike leaves; 'Variegata' has white-edged foliage. 'Boetica' grows especially upright to 4 to 6 feet, with heavy, twisted, picturesque branches. 'Compacta' is dense and slow-growing, eventually reaching about 3 feet high, with proportionally smaller leaves; leaves of 'Compacta Variegata' are rimmed in white. Smaller than any of these is *M. c.* 'Microphylla', with tiny, almost scalelike leaves.

Myrtles are amenable shrubs that will prosper from seashore to desert, in sun or partial shade. Leaves will show tip burn if roots are kept too moist.

NANDINA DOMESTICA

H E A V E N L Y   B A M B O O

Pictured above left

Zones: 8–10 (West), 8 and 9 (East)
Growth rate: Slow to moderate, to 8 feet
Soil: Prefers well-drained soil
Water: Prefers regular watering; established plants are drought-tolerant
Exposure: Sun to shade

"Feathery" is the word for heavenly bamboo. Stems rise vertically from the ground, bearing—almost at right angles—large leaves composed of countless narrow, pointed leaflets. New growth is pink- or bronze-tinged, later becoming a fresh, lettucelike green; cool autumn weather brings reddish tones to the foliage, and in winter, the entire plant often turns brilliant red. Airy pyramidal clusters of tiny, creamy-white flowers bloom in middle to late spring; if another plant is nearby for pollination, blooms are followed by pea-size berries that become bright red in autumn.

Heavenly bamboo's bulk increases over the years as additional stems grow from the ground; you can increase bushiness and maintain foliage low on the plant (though the effect always will be vertical) by selectively cutting back stems to various heights to induce branching. Nurseries sometimes offer named selections and frequently carry dwarf varieties ('Harbour Dwarf', 'Nana') that are useful as ground covers for small areas.

Though winter foliage is more colorful on plants grown in full sun, heavenly bamboo will grow in partial shade anywhere—and needs it where summers are hot and dry. Leaves may become chlorotic on plants in alkaline soil.

NERIUM OLEANDER

O L E A N D E R

Pictured on page 36

Zones: 9 and 10
Growth rate: Moderate to fast, to 8–12 feet
Soil: Not particular
Water: Needs moderate watering when young; established plants are drought-tolerant
Exposure: Sun

Oleander seems to thrive in just about any climate; only cool, foggy gardens will see it looking second-best. Overall appearance is coarse-textured: many stems rise from the ground to form a rounded shrub bearing thick, lance-shaped, glossy leaves to 12 inches long on vigorous shoots. You can use oleander as a specimen shrub or informal (or even shaped) hedge or barrier, or train as a small tree with one or several trunks. Flowering begins in mid to late spring and lasts into autumn; 2- to 3-inch blossoms are borne in showy clusters at branch ends. Many named varieties are available, with single or double flowers (some fragrant) in white, pink, salmon, yellow, red. Varieties in the 'Petite' series are smaller plants (to about 4 feet); at the other end of the scale is the popular white 'Sister Agnes', which will reach 20 feet. Semidwarf varieties—to about 6 feet tall—include 'Algiers' and 'Little Red' (red), 'Tangier' (pink), and 'Casablanca' (white).

Though oleanders grow well in a variety of soils, they should receive regular to moderate watering during their first several years, until roots are well established. Aphids and scale may be occasional pests. Bacterial gall sometimes causes cankers on young stems and galls on older growth; to control, cut off stems well below visible infection.

CAUTION: All parts of the oleander plant are poisonous if ingested; smoke from burning branches can cause severe respiratory irritation.

OSMANTHUS

Zones: Vary
Growth rate: Slow to moderate, to various heights
Soil: Not particular
Water: Needs moderate watering; established plants tolerate occasional watering
Exposure: Sun; partial shade in hot-summer regions

Dense, orderly growth and glossy foliage recommend the various osmanthus species as good "basic" shrubs—but the deliciously fragrant (though usually inconspicuous) flowers elevate these plants beyond the strictly useful.

Sweet olive, *O. fragrans* (Zones 9 and 10), possesses the most penetrating fragrance of all: sweet and fruity, detectable for some distance from the plant. Its tiny white blossoms appear primarily in spring and summer, but also bloom sporadically during the rest of the year. Glossy, oval leaves are about 4 inches long. *O. fragrans* eventually becomes a mounded shrub to 10 or more feet high and wide, but occasional pruning can limit height and spread.

Delavay osmanthus, *O. delavayi* (Zones 8–10), is another species with a mounding growth habit, reaching 6 feet tall with greater spread. Branches are arching; inch-long leaves give the shrub a fine-textured look. Early to midspring white flowers are somewhat showy.

Holly-leaf osmanthus, *O. heterophyllus* (Zones 7–10), is sometimes sold as *O. aquifolium* or *O. ilicifolius*. The 2½-inch, spine-edged leaves suggest those of English holly (*Ilex aquifolium*), and the late autumn and winter flowers form small fruits—but they're blue-black rather than red. Habit is dome-shaped, with an ultimate height of about 20 feet if growth is unrestricted. Varieties 'Gulftide' and 'Ilicifolius' are more upright; 'Purpureus' has purple new growth, while 'Variegatus' (reaching only 4 to 5 feet) has ivory-edged leaves.

PINUS MUGO MUGO

M U G H O   P I N E

Zones: 3–10 (West), 3–8 (East)
Growth rate: Slow, to 4 feet
Soil: Needs well-drained soil
Water: Needs moderate watering
Exposure: Sun to partial shade

In contrast to tall and stalwart pine trees, Mugho pine is a small, somewhat billowy shrub with stuffed-animal charm. Branches tend to be spreading with upturned tips, clothed in paired needles to 2 inches long. Among plants raised from seed, needle length varies from plant to plant; those with shorter needles are slower-growing, smaller, and denser. In time, Mugho pine's width usually exceeds its height. You can limit growth (and achieve a bushier plant) by selectively cutting back new growth in spring. A single Mugho pine makes an attractive accent; a row will serve as as low hedge.

PITTOSPORUM TOBIRA

T O B I R A

Pictured on page 37

Zones: 8–10
Growth rate: Moderate, to 6–15 feet
Soil: Prefers well-drained soil
Water: Prefers regular watering; tolerates moderate watering
Exposure: Sun to partial shade

Here is a rugged, versatile shrub (or even small tree) for an individual accent, informal hedge, or mass planting. Tobira is mound-shaped or rounded, densely covered in leathery, highly polished, dark green leaves that are carried radially around the stems, clustering toward branch tips. Each blunt-tipped, rather narrow leaf is up to 5 inches long. Creamy-white flowers, with a scent like

---

Shade-tolerant Shrubs

(D) Deciduous; (E) Evergreen

Aucuba japonica (E)	**Nandina domestica (E)**
Camellia (E)	**Osmanthus (E)**
Clethra alnifolia (D)	**Pittosporum (E)**
Euonymus fortunei (E)	**Rhododendron (E)**
Ilex (E)	**Taxus (E)**
Ligustrum japonicum (E)	**Viburnum davidii (E)**

... **Pittosporum tobira**

that of orange blossoms, bloom in early spring, followed by fruits the size of large peas. Fruits split open in autumn to reveal sticky orange seeds.

Variety 'Variegata' usually remains under 6 feet high and wide; its gray-green leaves, irregularly margined and washed with white and ivory, add an especially attractive, light-colored accent to shady spots. 'Wheeler's Dwarf', just 2 feet tall, is a scaled-down version of the species.

Once tobira is established, it will perform well with moderate watering; in cool-summer regions, it qualifies as drought-tolerant. Aphids can be a periodic pest; scale may appear occasionally.

RAPHIOLEPIS INDICA

I N D I A   H A W T H O R N

Zones: 8–10
Growth rate: Slow to moderate, to various heights
Soil: Needs well-drained soil
Water: Needs moderate watering
Exposure: Sun

Handsome, leathery foliage, neat and compact growth, quantities of attractive flowers from winter to late spring—these sterling qualities have led to virtual overplanting of this fine shrub. But as countless public and commercial landscapes testify, India hawthorn is an ideal choice for the easy-care garden.

Nurseries now carry many named varieties differing in size, shape, and flower color. All feature broadly oval, pointed, 1½- to 3-inch-long leaves (usually red- or bronze-tinted when new) and ½-inch blossoms in dense clusters. Among the tallest—to 6 feet—are 'Rosea' (light to medium pink flowers, rounded plant), 'Springtime' (deep pink, upright), and 'Bill Evans' (large, light

Azalea hybrids

pink flowers; fast-growing, open plant). Shorter, to 4 to 5 feet, are 'Clara' (white flowers, rounded form), 'Enchantress' (deep pink, fairly fast-growing), 'Jack Evans' (pink, spreading), 'Pink Lady' (deep pink, rounded), and 'Snow White' (white, spreading). Lowest growers include 'Ballerina' (deep pink flowers, spreading form), 'Coates Crimson' (dark pink, rounded), 'Fascination' (pink and white, rounded), and 'Rosea Dwarf' (light pink, rounded).

In desert gardens, plants need light shade during the heat of summer days to avoid sunburn. Aphids are an occasional pest; fungus leaf spot may appear during cold, wet times of year.

RHODODENDRON

R H O D O D E N D R O N

A Z A L E A

Pictured above

Zones: Vary
Growth rate: Slow to moderate, to various heights
Soil: Needs well-drained, slightly acid soil
Water: Needs regular watering
Exposure: Shade, partial shade, or sun

Rhododendrons and azaleas aren't everyone's easy-care plants: their soil and climate requirements limit their general use to regions where these conditions exist naturally or are easy to achieve. But where they are acclimated, they are basic landscape shrubs, cher-

---

Drought-tolerant Shrubs

(D) Deciduous; (E) Evergreen

Aucuba japonica (E)	**Dodonaea viscosa (E)**
Caragana arborescens (D)	**Elaeagnus (E)**
Chaenomeles (D)	**Myrtus communis (E)**
Cistus (E)	**Nerium oleander (E)**
Cotinus coggygria (D)	**Taxus (E)**

ished for lavish floral displays in a great range of colors and color combinations.

Rhododendrons. Rhododendrons exhibit astonishing variety in shape and size, ranging from tree-size shrubs with volleyball-size flower clusters to ground-hugging creepers with blossoms and leaves under an inch in size. Physical differences aside, they share a need for regular watering and acid, well-drained soil high in organic matter. Beyond this, they thrive where the atmosphere is cool and humid. Natural rhododendron country includes the Pacific Northwest (west of the Cascades) and down the California coast to below San Francisco; Appalachian highlands from northern Georgia into New York; the Atlantic seaboard from northern Delaware through New England; and areas westward through New York, Pennsylvania, and parts of Ohio (especially near Lake Erie). Though these regions encompass a range of low winter temperatures, there are rhododendron varieties suitable for each. To learn which types are best for your area, visit public gardens and well-stocked nurseries.

Azaleas. In the South, evergreen azaleas have been a mainstay of graceful landscapes for generations. Because they can withstand more heat than rhododendrons, azaleas grow well in not only the areas outlined for rhododendrons, but also in much of California (except desert and mountain areas) plus the Middle and Deep South. Many hybrid groups have been developed, and many varieties are available in each group; plant and flower size vary, as do low-temperature tolerances. For azaleas, as

Viburnum davidii

for rhododendrons, your best selection guide is a visit to a local nursery or public garden.

TAXUS

Y E W

Zones: Vary
Growth rate: Slow, to various heights
Soil: Needs well-drained soil
Water: Needs moderate watering when young; established plants are drought-tolerant
Exposure: Sun to partial shade

Yews are the classic topiary plant, an essential component of formal gardens. But they're far more versatile than the traditional uses suggest: they make excellent hedges, screens, backgrounds, and foundation plantings. Slow-growing and easy to manage, they'll take any amount of shearing or none at all. Growth habit may be upright, spreading, or in between; short, flattened needles densely cover the branches.

Nurseries offer varieties of three yew species. Female trees bear decorative, cup-shaped, usually red fruits; the seeds they contain, and yew foliage, are poisonous.

English yew, *T. baccata* (Zones 6–9), is well known through several widely planted varieties. *T. b.* 'Stricta', the Irish yew, forms a broad, flat-topped column reaching 20 feet or more; branches are upright, spreading outward at the top. 'Stricta Aurea' has yellow new growth, while 'Stricta Variegata' features cream-variegated needles. 'Erecta' is more narrowly upright and less dense than 'Stricta', with shorter needles. 'Repandens', the spreading English yew, is a good choice for a low foundation plant or ground cover—it may spread to 6 feet wide but reaches only 2 feet tall. 'Repandens Aurea' has yellow new growth. Midway between upright and spreading in habit is 'Adpressa', which reaches 5 feet in both directions; its ½-inch needles give it a finer texture than the other varieties.

Japanese yew, *T. cuspidata* (Zones 5–9), also has upright and spreading varieties. 'Capitata' forms a dense pyramid that may attain a height of 25 feet after many years; 'Nana' spreads widely but remains 3 to 4 feet tall; 'Densiformis' is in the same height range but spreads to only about twice its height.

The varieties of *T. media* (Zones 5–9) are hybrids of English and Japanese yew. Slimmest of the upright types is 'Hicksii', growing to about 12 feet tall. 'Hatfieldii' reaches about the same

height but forms a thicker, broader-based column. 'Brownii' is a rounded plant 4 to 8 feet tall.

Yew foliage will be sunburned if exposed to reflected heat in summer and can be damaged in cold-winter areas if not protected from bright sunlight and wind. Spider mites and scale are occasional pests; black vine weevils can attack roots.

VIBURNUM

Pictured below left

Zones: 8–10
Growth rate: Varies
Soil: Needs good, well-drained soil
Water: Needs regular watering
Exposure: Varies

Two evergreen viburnums are noted for especially handsome foliage and orderly growth. Slow-growing *V. davidii* is a good choice for shaded and semishaded locations where you need a low, spreading plant. This species may reach 3 feet tall and spread a bit wider; it's attractive as an accent plant and excellent when massed as a high ground cover or planted as a low hedge. Broadly oval leaves to 6 inches long have distinct longitudinal veining; spring flowers aren't showy, though clusters of attractive blue-green, rounded fruits may follow.

Neat, dense growth makes *V. tinus* (laurustinus) a good-looking specimen shrub and also recommends it for hedge and screen planting. Foliage, flowers, and fruits are all attractive. The basic species is broadly upright, growing at a moderate rate to 10 to 12 feet tall, 5 to 8 feet wide. Dark green, oval, 3-inch leaves create a dense foliage cover. Clusters of white flowers open from pink buds in late autumn to early spring; flowers are followed by round, metallic blue fruits.

V. tinus varieties sold in the nursery trade include 'Variegatum', its foliage variegated with white and cream; 'Robustum' and 'Lucidum', larger-leafed and more mildew-resistant than the species; 'Spring Bouquet', with smaller foliage on a half-size plant; and 'Dwarf', a rounded shrub to about 5 feet tall and wide.

Laurustinus and its varieties will grow in sun where summers are cool but prefer partial shade in warmer regions. Foliage is susceptible to mildew in cool, humid weather and in coastal gardens.

Both *V. davidii* and *V. tinus* may be bothered occasionally by aphids and spider mites.

Consider Climate & Care in Planning Your Lawn

You can walk, play, and picnic on almost any outdoor surface, but only a lawn gives you softness, coolness, and that memorable grassy aroma. And though there's no denying that a lawn will top the garden maintenance list, countless homeowners feel that the rewards are worth the extra effort.

Choosing the grass

Selecting the right grass or blend of grasses for your climate is the first step toward achieving a successful lawn. In broad terms, there are two types of lawn grasses: cool-season and subtropical. Cool-season types—bluegrass, bent, fescue, and rye—flourish where winters are chilly or cold and summers aren't too hot and humid. Subtropicals, including Bermuda and zoysia, grow luxuriantly during hot weather but are dormant during the coldest months. For parts of semi-arid and arid western North America, a drought-tolerant grass may be the best choice; various types are available.

In addition to climate, consider the conditions in your garden. Some grasses are shade-tolerant; others must have sunshine. And some, especially subtropical and drought-tolerant types, spread aggressively by runners. This habit may add time to your maintenance schedule, particularly if your lawn isn't bordered by mowing strips.

Finally, weigh the benefits of a single grass versus a mixture before making your decision. A one-grass lawn will have a more uniform look, but a blended-grass lawn may be able to maintain good appearance even if pests or diseases afflict one of its components.

For help in selecting the best grass or grasses for your area, consult regional and local agencies. State and county agricultural extension services generally offer printed material for a nominal charge; personnel at reputable nurseries and garden centers can also advise you. For a thorough treatment of lawns, from grass selection to installation, refer to Sunset's *Lawns & Ground Covers*.

Easy-care layouts

If you want a lawn, you can't escape mowing and edging, but the simpler the lawn's layout, the easier these tasks will be to perform. Perhaps the simplest lawn to groom is a square or rectangular plot that can be mowed back and forth in overlapping strips. If you prefer a freeform lawn, design one with broadly sweeping curves and undulations so you won't have to maneuver the mower around tight bends. Keep the turf free of obstructions—every tree, shrub, or small planting bed interrupts the smooth flow of mowing and introduces more edges to clip.

Both mowing and edging can be simplified by the installation of mowing strips—solid, narrow borders (frequently of brick or concrete) that form the lawn's perimeter, provide solid footing for mower wheels, and function as a guide for all edging tools.

Installation

Adequate advance preparation is the crucial first step to a healthy lawn. Begin by grading the surface and preparing the soil (see pages 82 and 84) to provide a base for good root growth and an even surface for easier maintenance. This is also the time to select and install a watering system; types

Routine mowing of play-yard lawn is simplified by two design features: rectangular layout and concrete mowing strip. Landscape architect: Taro Yamagami.

of systems, sprinkler options, and such labor-saving accessories as timers are described on pages 85 to 89.

Though lawns are traditionally planted from seed, you should consider the pros and cons of seed-sowing, planting from plugs or stolons, and setting in sod. Planting from seed allows you the widest choice in grass types and blends, but the young lawn will need frequent attention—plenty of watering, as well as weed control—until roots are established and the turf fills in. To minimize or eliminate weeds in a new lawn, you can treat the unplanted soil with a preemergence herbicide or have it fumigated, then sow grass seed after the prescribed waiting period. Or water the soil and destroy germinating weeds by tilling or applying a contact herbicide, repeating the procedure until germination stops or is greatly reduced.

Some grasses, notably hybrid Bermuda grasses and zoysias, are planted from stolons or small plugs of turf. Lawns planted in this manner need the same thorough preparation and preplanting weed control required for lawns grown from seed; they also need regular watering until the lawn surface is filled in. In addition, it's a good idea to mulch the bare patches of ground between plugs to conserve moisture and discourage weeds.

If you plant rolls of sod purchased from a turf farm, you'll get an instant lawn that doesn't need the careful watering required by a seeded lawn. Elimination of weeds in the soil is likewise unnecessary, since the sod completely covers the ground, preventing germination. Compared to seeding, however, the cost is significantly higher, and your turf choices are likely to be more limited.

Choose a lawn grass *that's compatible with your climate and the intended use. This is durable, attractive perennial rye.*

Maintenance

The secret to any good lawn is regular care, and the secret to an easy-care lawn is efficiency. Itemize the maintenance routines and note their frequency; then take advantage of every time- and labor-saving device available.

As mentioned above, streamlining the yard's layout will lessen the time spent on chores such as mowing and edging; you can often speed things up further by relying on automatic tools rather than doing the work by hand. Regular watering, a virtual necessity for a healthy lawn, ceases to be a time-consuming duty if you install a sprinkler system and an automatic controller. Fertilizing, too, can be made easier: use a controlled-release fertilizer (see page 92) and apply it with a spreader. And coping with weeds, pests, and diseases should be necessary only occasionally, especially if you've prepared your lawn bed thoroughly and planted a grass or grass blend suitable for your climate.

Vines & Ground Covers Provide a Finishing Touch

V ines and ground covers aren't necessary components of every garden, but they often add just the right finishing touch. A carefully chosen vine can cover an otherwise monotonous surface with a filigree tracery—a touch of greenery that joins the structure to the landscape. Ground covers serve much the same purpose on a horizontal plane, uniting a landscape and providing a low, uniform alternative to a grassy lawn.

In selecting easy-care vines, we have focused on those that don't need frequent thinning, training, or pruning. But virtually all vines require *some* training: those that climb by twining or tendrils may need untangling, redirection, or thinning, while clingers—those with aerial rootlets or sucker discs—need watching so they won't attach themselves where they're not wanted. And vines having no means of attachment must be tied into place. A few of our choices—wisteria, for example—do need attentive guidance during the growing season (particularly during their early years) and some annual thinning or pruning, but are so beautiful and useful that this maintenance may well seem worthwhile.

Among ground covers, you'll find low-spreading shrubs, vines, and perennials that grow in either vinelike or clumping forms. These easy-care selections will maintain their good looks with little pruning, mowing, restriction of roots and stems, or replanting.

Basic landscape of the garden at far left relies entirely on one vine and one ground cover. Other photos include fragrant star jasmine (Trachelospermum jasminoides, top center), soft gray lavender cotton (Santolina chamaecyparissus, top right) and flashy trailing African daisy (Osteospermum fruticosum, bottom)

Bougainvillea 'San Diego Red'

BOUGAINVILLEA

Pictured above

Zones: 10 (9 and 10 for *B. spectabilis*)
Type: Evergreen to partially deciduous
Growth rate: Fast, to 15–30 feet
Soil: Not particular
Water: Needs regular to periodic watering
Exposure: Sun to light shade
How it climbs: Must be tied

A bougainvillea in bloom is nothing less than flamboyant. The true flowers are inconspicuous, but the papery, petal-like bracts that surround them put on a dazzling show in tropical, neon-bright colors: purple, magenta, crimson, brick red, orange, yellow, pink, or white. Many named selections are available, including several shrubby varieties that make good container plants. The peak flowering period comes in summer, but blooms may appear from spring through autumn (even into winter) in the mildest climates. Once established, bougainvilleas quickly recover from light frosts; purple-flowered *B. spectabilis* grows throughout most of Zone 9.

Bougainvillea is a fast, vigorous grower, reaching 15 to 30 feet depending on the variety. Its stiff stems, armed with long, sharp, needlelike thorns, are moderately clothed in medium green, heart-shaped leaves to 2½ inches long. Use this vine as a spectacular wall or trellis display, or to cover an overhead structure (even a roof); or plant it on a bank as a high ground cover.

Set out plants in spring; choose a sunny location except in the hottest areas, where plants may appreciate partial or afternoon shade. Water regularly during the spring growth period, periodically thereafter. Prune in early spring to shape, thin, and control; pinch or head back stems during spring and summer as needed to direct growth.

CLEMATIS

Pictured on facing page

Zones: 5–9
Type: Deciduous
Growth rate: Fast, to 20–30 feet
Soil: Needs good, well-drained, nonacid soil
Water: Needs regular watering
Exposure: Sun to partial shade
How it climbs: Twining leaf stalks

Though the familiar large-flowered clematis hybrids require too much pruning and fertilizing to qualify as easy-care, two clematis species do fit comfortably into a low-maintenance scheme. Anemone clematis, *C. montana*, puts on a lavish floral display in early spring just before leaves emerge. The four-petaled, 2½-inch flowers resemble Japanese anemone; color is white, turning to pink

with age. A pink-flowering form, *C. m. rubens*, opens rosy red and fades to pink; emerging new foliage is bronzy red. For pink flowers to 4 inches across, look for variety 'Tetrarose'. Fluffy seed heads provide a restrained summer show.

Anemone clematis grows vigorously to at least 20 feet; leaves are 3 to 4 inches long, each consisting of three pointed oval leaflets. Besides adorning fences, walls, overheads, and eaves, this clematis looks attractive twining around tree trunks and branches.

Sweet autumn clematis, *C. dioscoreifolia* (frequently sold as *C. paniculata*), offers frothy masses of small, fragrant white flowers against a backdrop of glossy dark green leaves in late summer and into autumn. Each leaf consists of three to five oval leaflets up to 2½ inches long; in milder regions, foliage is partially evergreen. Vigorous vines quickly reach 20 to 30 feet; uses are the same as for anemone clematis.

Both these species need some annual pruning to thin, direct, or contain growth. Prune anemone clematis right after flowering—blooms come on stems formed the previous year. Prune sweet autumn clematis just after bloom or in early spring before new growth begins.

EUONYMUS FORTUNEI

W I N T E R   C R E E P E R

Zones: 5–10
Type: Evergreen
Growth rate: Moderate, to 20 feet
Soil: Not particular
Water: Needs moderate watering
Exposure: Sun to shade
How it climbs: Clinging

Depending on how you use it and on the selected variety you plant, *E. fortunei* can be a vine, ground cover, or shrub (page 44). In all climbing or trailing forms, stems have rootlets that cling to vertical surfaces or root in moist soil.

The basic species bears dark green, oval leaves to 2½ inches long on stems that trail or climb to 20 feet or more in the plant's juvenile phase. Mature vines send out short, shrubby branches that bear decorative orange fruit capsules resembling tiny hatboxes. More widely available in the nursery trade is common winter creeper, *E. f. radicans* (sometimes sold as *E. radicans*). It's smaller-foliaged than the species, with leaves just 1 inch long.

E. f. 'Colorata', purple-leaf winter creeper, looks much like *E. f. radicans*, but its leaves turn purple in autumn (and stay that way in winter). Variety

'Kewensis' ('Minima') reaches just 4 feet; its tiny (¼-inch) leaves give it a fine-textured look. Big-leaf winter creeper, *E. f.* 'Vegeta', is a somewhat shrubby plant that will cling to vertical surfaces (including tree trunks); leaves are leathery and rounded, to 1¼ inches. Mature vines of this variety produce short stems bearing pink and orange fruits in autumn.

GELSEMIUM SEMPERVIRENS

CAROLINA JESSAMINE

Pictured at right

Zones: 8–10
Type: Evergreen
Growth rate: Moderate, to 20 feet
Soil: Needs good, well-drained soil
Water: Needs regular watering
Exposure: Sun to light shade
How it climbs: Twining

Delicacy and restraint mark the Carolina jessamine. Slender, reddish-brown stems, bearing paired shiny, yellowish-green, oval leaves to 4 inches long, twine loosely to form a filigree cover on vertical surfaces or spill gracefully from a pergola, wall top, or planter edge. Given no support, they'll spread out to form a high ground cover. Fragrant,

Clematis montana

trumpet-shaped, bright yellow blossoms to 1½ inches long appear in the cooler months. Winter and early spring are the main flowering seasons, but in the warmest climates, the vines may bloom from November into May.

Carolina jessamine may need some annual thinning or pruning, done after the flowering period.

CAUTION: All parts of this plant are poisonous if ingested.

HEDERA

IVY

Zones: Vary
Type: Evergreen
Growth rate: Moderate, to indefinite size
Soil: Not particular
Water: Prefers regular watering; tolerates moderate watering
Exposure: Sun to shade
How it climbs: Clinging

Vigor, adaptability, and versatility are three characteristics that make ivy an outstanding easy-care choice. It thrives in sun (except in the desert) or shade; it grows equally well as a vine or a ground cover. Either way, the foliage cover is dense and even. Grown as a vine, ivy holds fast to virtually any surface with its aerial rootlets; in fairly short order, it can interlace and entirely obscure a chain link or wire fence. Be sure to plant ivy only where you won't want it removed—you don't direct this vine's growth, you simply confine it to areas where it is wanted.

After a number of years, vines will produce short, shrubby mature stems bearing clusters of insignificant greenish flowers followed by small black berries. Mature leaves are broadly oval, without the lobes of normal vining foliage.

English ivy, *H. helix*, is the more widely grown of the two most common species. Zones 5–10 are the reliable growing regions, though several selections ('Baltica' is the most widely distributed) will survive in Zone 4, especially if planted in a sheltered location. In Zones 5–7, English ivy needs some shade during winter to prevent sunburn.

English ivy's three- to five-lobed leaves are roughly diamond-shaped, ranging from 2 to 4 inches wide and long. The typical color is dark green with paler veins, but numerous fancy-leafed types are also sold—some with yellow or white variegation, others with different leaf shapes, and almost all with smaller foliage than the species. These fancy forms won't cover as large

Gelsemium sempervirens

an expanse as the basic species will, but they're good for smaller areas.

Algerian ivy, *H. canariensis*, thrives in Zones 9 and 10, where you'll often see mile after mile of it covering the slopes adjoining freeways. Glossy, medium green, three- to five-lobed leaves are 5 to 8 inches wide and long. At least one variegated form is widely grown; its leaves are irregularly edged in creamy white.

To limit growth of either English or Algerian ivy, head back or remove stems at any time of year. In humid-summer regions, leaf spot may occur, usually in ground cover plantings.

HIBBERTIA SCANDENS

GUINEA GOLD VINE

Zones: 10 and warmest parts of 9
Type: Evergreen
Growth rate: Fast, to 10 feet
Soil: Needs well-drained soil
Water: Needs regular watering
Exposure: Sun to partial shade
How it climbs: Twining

For grace, elegance, and brilliant bloom, choose Guinea gold vine. The twining stems quickly reach up to 10 feet, but the plant doesn't grow out of control or become unmanageably tangled. Foliage alone is good-looking: dark green,

. . . Hibbertia scandens

glossy, oval leaves up to 3 inches long. From midspring into autumn, the vines bear bright yellow, 3-inch-wide blossoms resembling single roses.

Plant Guinea gold vine in sun (but not against a wall that reflects heat) or partial shade. Prune and thin out stems in early spring before flowers appear.

JASMINUM

J A S M I N E

Zones: Vary
Type: Evergreen, semi-evergreen, and deciduous
Growth rate: Moderate to fast, to various sizes
Soil: Needs well-drained soil
Water: Needs regular watering
Exposure: Sun to partial shade
How it climbs: Varies

Four climbing jasmines suit an easy-care garden; all share the virtue of heavenly fragrance. Spanish jasmine, *J. grandiflorum* (Zones 9 and 10), loses part to all of its foliage in frosty-winter areas. Glossy leaves consist of five to seven narrow, 2-inch leaflets; clusters of star-shaped white flowers to 1½ inches wide appear throughout summer. Growth is fast, to 15 to 20 feet; vines must be tied in place.

Angelwing jasmine (*J. nitidum*, sometimes sold as *J. magnificum*) grows in Zone 10 and the warmest parts of Zone 9. Except in frost-free areas, its leathery, 2-inch-long, pointed oval leaves are partially deciduous. From late spring into summer, 1-inch-wide, pinwheel-shaped flowers—white with purple petal undersides—bloom in clusters. This vine grows moderately rapidly to 10 to 20 feet; stems must be tied.

Common white jasmine, *J. officinale* (Zones 9 and 10), resembles Spanish jasmine but has slightly smaller flowers on a larger plant that will twine to 30 feet. It, too, loses some of its foliage in colder regions. Evergreen *J. polyanthum* (Zones 9 and 10) rapidly twines to 20 feet or more. Many narrow leaflets—five to seven per leaf—give the plant a fine texture. Clusters of white flowers with pink-backed petals appear from late winter to summer in the mildest regions, in spring where weather is colder.

You'll need to do some thinning and pruning each year to keep vines attractive. Do this after flowering, since plants bloom on stems produced the previous year.

LONICERA

H O N E Y S U C K L E

Pictured below left

Zones: Vary
Type: Evergreen to deciduous
Growth rate: Moderate to fast, to various sizes
Soil: Not particular
Water: Needs regular watering
Exposure: Sun to partial shade
How it climbs: Twining

Some of the more widely planted honeysuckles, such as *L. japonica* and *L. sempervirens*, grow so rampantly that they become maintenance problems. The following choices, though, have more orderly growth. All have flaring tubular flowers; leaves grow in pairs on opposite sides of the stems.

Gold flame honeysuckle, *L. heckrottii* (Zones 5–10), flowers from spring into autumn, showing off its fragrant blooms against a backdrop of blue-green leaves. Clusters of 1½-inch-long, coral-pink buds open to reveal yellow interiors. This plant is a somewhat shrubby climber that will extend to 15 feet; it's partially deciduous in warmer zones, entirely deciduous elsewhere.

Though it resembles ultra-vigorous *L. japonica*, *L. henryi* is a much more restrained grower (to about 15 feet) in Zones 5–10; in Zone 5, it loses its leaves in winter, but in other regions it's largely or entirely evergreen. Fragrant yellowish- to purplish-red paired flowers, slightly under an inch long, are followed by small blue-black berries.

Deciduous *L. periclymenum* (Zones 5–9) is usually offered in the selected form 'Serotina'—more restrained in growth (to 15 feet) than the species. Fragrant, creamy white blossoms open from red buds from summer into autumn; red berries follow the flowers. The deciduous to semideciduous hybrid *L.* 'Dropmore Scarlet' (Zones 3–10) also flowers from summer into autumn; blossoms of this 15-foot vine are solid bright red.

Lonicera hildebrandiana

Colorful Flowering Vines

Bougainvillea
White, pink, red, purple, orange, yellow

Clematis
White, pink

Gelsemium sempervirens
Yellow

Hibbertia scandens
Yellow

Jasminum
White

Lonicera
Yellow, pink, red

Mandevilla laxa
White

Solanum jasminoides
White

Tecomaria capensis
Red-orange, yellow

Trachelospermum jasminoides
White

Wisteria
Lavender, purple, pink, white

Largest of the group is giant Burmese honeysuckle, *L. hildebrandiana* (Zones 9 and 10). Rapid growth to about 30 feet produces thick stems and glossy, dark green, oval leaves to 6 inches long. Fragrant summer flowers up to 7 inches long are white when they open, turning chamois yellow to soft orange as they age. Burmese honeysuckle grows less densely than other honeysuckles; use it for its strong character on a wall or fence, or on overhead structures.

Honeysuckles thrive in sun where summers are mild but prefer a bit of shade in hot-summer regions. Aphids may be an occasional problem.

MANDEVILLA LAXA

CHILEAN JASMINE

Zones: 8–10
Type: Deciduous
Growth rate: Moderate, to 15 feet
Soil: Needs good, well-drained soil
Water: Needs regular watering
Exposure: Sun
How it climbs: Twining

Despite the common name, *M. laxa*'s powerfully fragrant summer flowers have a scent more reminiscent of gardenias than jasmine. Each tubular white blossom flares out to a 2-inch-wide star. Slender stems twine vigorously; deep green, oblong leaves to 6 inches long have heart-shaped bases. Some nurseries sell this plant as *M. suaveolens*.

Prune to thin or untangle stems in late winter before growth starts. If stems are frost-damaged in Zone 8, cut out damaged stems; plant will regrow quickly.

PARTHENOCISSUS

Pictured above right

Zones: Vary
Type: Deciduous
Growth rate: Moderate to fast, to indefinite size
Soil: Prefers good, well-drained soil
Water: Prefers regular watering
Exposure: Sun to partial shade
How it climbs: Varies

Though notably attractive during their leafy period, the two *Parthenocissus* species described here have earned a special reputation for smashing autumn colors of orange, red, and purple. Both species bear clusters of small, bluish-black autumn fruits resembling bunches of tiny grapes.

Boston ivy, *P. tricuspidata* (Zones 4–10), has three-lobed leaves that vary a bit in shape and size, reaching up to 8 inches across. Stems cling tenaciously with small roots to nearly any surface, forming an even cover of overlapping foliage. The extent of coverage is seemingly limitless—the larger the wall, the farther the vine will travel. Two small-leafed selections, 'Lowii' and 'Veitchii', are vigorous but cover considerably less territory. (Avoid planting Boston ivy near wood or shingle siding, since it can accelerate the deterioration of wood and grow between shingles.)

Virginia creeper, *P. quinquefolia* (Zones 3–10), is among the first plants to change color in autumn. Each leaf is divided into five pointed, 6-inch leaflets. This is a vigorous vine that will climb or scramble great distances if unrestricted—but because its foliage cover is less dense than that of Boston ivy, it decorates surfaces rather than obscures them. It's a better choice than Boston ivy for arbors and other overhead structures.

Virginia creeper attaches itself with disc-tipped tendrils and often needs some initial support or tying. Variety 'Engelmannii' has smaller leaves and a denser foliage cover than the basic species.

Both Boston ivy and Virginia creeper grow best in good soil with regular watering, but will still look respectable in less than ideal situations. Some shade is needed in regions with hot, dry summers. Prune or thin as necessary to control size or direct growth.

SOLANUM JASMINOIDES

POTATO VINE

Zones: 9 and 10
Type: Evergreen to partially deciduous
Growth rate: Fast, to 30 feet
Soil: Needs well-drained soil
Water: Prefers regular watering
Exposure: Sun to partial shade
How it climbs: Twining

Though its principal flowering period is in spring, potato vine may bloom at any time of year when weather is mild. The star-shaped, inch-wide flowers, each hanging from a threadlike stalk, are borne in clusters of 8 to 12; each white to bluish-white bloom has a yellow center. Arrow-shaped leaves to 3 inches long are green or purple-tinted, partially deciduous where there is winter frost.

The overall effect of this vine is delicate and frothy, yet it's almost rampant and needs periodic thinning to prevent

Parthenocissus quinquefolia

it from becoming a tangled mass of stems (you can prune or thin in any season). Plant potato vine in sun where summers are mild, in partial shade in warmer regions.

TECOMARIA CAPENSIS

CAPE HONEYSUCKLE

Zones: 9 and 10
Type: Evergreen
Growth rate: Moderate to fast, to 25 feet
Soil: Prefers well-drained soil
Water: Needs moderate watering when young; established plants are somewhat drought-tolerant
Exposure: Sun to partial shade
How it climbs: Must be tied

Here is a truly multipurpose plant: it can serve as vine, ground cover, or, with pruning, shrub. As a vigorous

. . . Tecomaria capensis

vine, it will extend to 25 feet, providing flashy color during summer and autumn. Tubular flowers resembling honeysuckle blossoms appear in brilliant red-orange clusters at branch tips. The plentiful foliage is a lustrous dark green; each leaf is composed of many small, rounded leaflets, giving the vine an overall fine-textured appearance. Variety 'Aurea' is a somewhat smaller, slower-growing type with yellow flowers and lighter foliage.

Cape honeysuckle tolerates a variety of conditions, including desert heat, salty ocean air, and wind. It prefers well-drained soil but will grow in heavy clay if not overwatered. For the best blossom display, plant in full sun; in partial shade you'll get fine growth but fewer flowers. Do major pruning in winter after flowering is finished; light pruning to control or direct growth can be done at any time.

TRACHELOSPERMUM JASMINOIDES

STAR JASMINE

CONFEDERATE JASMINE

Pictured at right

Zones: 9 and 10
Type: Evergreen
Growth rate: Moderately fast, to 20 feet
Soil: Needs well-drained soil
Water: Needs regular watering
Exposure: Sun to partial shade
How it climbs: Twining

Versatility is one of star jasmine's virtues. Given support, it can climb up to 20 feet on a wall; with less training, it will twine around posts. If allowed to spread, it makes a first-rate ground cover to about 2 feet high; if confined, it will spill gracefully over the sides of raised planters or other containers. Leathery, oval leaves with pointed tips grow up to 3 inches long; dark green and glossy, they're attractive all year. From late spring into summer, the plant produces a heavy crop of inch-wide, pinwheel-shaped white flowers so intensely fragrant that the scent can be detected yards away.

Plant star jasmine in full sun where summers are mild, in partial shade in hot-summer regions. It appreciates fertilizer in early spring and at the end of the flowering period. Plants aren't usually bothered by pests but may occasionally be visited by scale, mealybugs, or spider mites. Chlorosis may occur where soil is alkaline.

Trachelospermum jasminoides

WISTERIA

Zones: 4–10
Type: Deciduous
Growth rate: Fast, to indefinite size
Soil: Needs well-drained soil
Water: Needs regular to periodic watering
Exposure: Sun to partial shade
How it climbs: Twining

Wisteria has earned international renown for its lavish and wonderfully fragrant early spring floral display. The two most widely planted species—Chinese and Japanese—differ in certain details. Chinese wisteria, *W. sinensis*, is the more commonly grown. Before leaf-out, foot-long hanging clusters of sweet pea–like lavender or white flowers burst forth from bare stems; all blossoms in a cluster open almost simultaneously. Some beanlike, pendant seed pods develop after flowers fade. Leaves are divided into elegantly narrow, pointed leaflets—seven to 13 per leaf. In autumn, foliage turns to tawny yellow.

Japanese wisteria, *W. floribunda* (sometimes sold as *W. multijuga*), has somewhat larger leaves than *W. sinensis*, with slightly broader and more numerous leaflets (15 to 19 per leaf). Foliage turns yellowish in autumn. Flowers are grouped in longer clusters—about 18 inches on the average, though 5-foot lengths have been recorded in Japan. For the longest clusters (to 3 feet), look for variety 'Macrobotrys'. Colors include lavender, purple, pink, and white; there's also a selection with double violet flowers. Single-flowered varieties may produce some hanging seed pods.

Water young wisteria plants regularly; older plants can get by with occasional watering, though they'll perform better with regular watering during and immediately after bloom. In alkaline soils, vines may become chlorotic.

In its early years, wisteria grows rampantly and needs consistent training and thinning to establish the woody framework you want; stems will twine around supports, branches of nearby plants, and each other. Give older plants an annual thinning and some heading back during the dormant period.

ARCTOSTAPHYLOS UVA-URSI

B E A R B E R R Y

K I N N I K I N N I C K

Zones: 3–10 (West), 3–7 (East)
Type: Evergreen
Growth rate: Moderate, spreading to 15 feet
Soil: Needs well-drained soil
Water: Prefers regular watering; established plants are drought-tolerant
Exposure: Sun to partial shade

Bearberry presents a neat, trim appearance in every season. Thick, oval leaves up to an inch long are glossy dark green, turning to bronzy red during the coldest months. Clusters of white to pinkish flowers in early spring are followed by small, berrylike fruits that turn red as they ripen (usually in summer).

Young bearberry plants are ground-hugging mats, eventually branching to make a cover up to 12 inches deep. Mulch young plantings to discourage weeds and to keep soil moist so stems in contact with the earth will root and spread easily.

In the wild, bearberry ranges from seashore to mountains, prospering in windswept locations and in poor soil. Established plants will tolerate considerable drought, especially where summers are cool. Nurseries may offer various named selections; 'Point Reyes' is a good choice for areas where summers are dry and warm to hot.

ARMERIA MARITIMA

See Perennials, page 66

BACCHARIS PILULARIS

C O Y O T E   B R U S H

D W A R F   C H A P A R R A L   B R O O M

Zones: 8–10 (West)
Type: Evergreen
Growth rate: Moderate to fast, spreading to 6–10 feet
Soil: Not particular; tolerates poorly drained soil
Water: Prefers moderate watering; established plants are drought-tolerant
Exposure: Sun

Here is a shrubby ground cover that will be right at home in almost any western garden, from seashore to high desert and in between. And in all but the hottest regions, it will survive—even prosper—with no supplemental watering.

Coyote brush grows to about 2 feet tall; an expanse planted with it will have an undulating surface densely covered in ½-inch leaves. To avoid planting flowering forms, which produce quantities of cottony, airborne seeds, choose one of the named selections: 'Twin Peaks' (also sold as 'Twin Peaks #2') and 'Pigeon Point' are generally available. 'Twin Peaks' has smaller, darker leaves and grows less rapidly than 'Pigeon Point'. To rejuvenate or tidy up established plantings, cut out old and erratically growing stems in late winter.

CONVALLARIA MAJALIS

L I L Y - O F - T H E - V A L L E Y

Pictured below

Zones: 3–9 (West), 3–7 (East)
Type: Deciduous
Growth rate: Slow, to indefinite spread
Soil: Needs good, well-drained soil
Water: Prefers regular watering
Exposure: Partial shade

If you need a refined, noninvasive ground cover for a lightly shaded patio or woodland-edge garden, lily-of-the-valley should be high among your considerations. An individual plant consists of two or three broadly oval, pointed leaves up to 8 inches long; underground rhizomes form gradually expanding clumps that create a thick carpet of foliage 6 to 10 inches high. In mid-

---

Colorful Flowering Ground Covers

- **Arctostaphylos uva-ursi**
  White, pink

- **Armeria maritima**
  Pink, white

- **Convallaria majalis**
  White

- **Cotoneaster**
  White, pink

- **Gazania**
  White, cream, yellow, orange, bronze, red, maroon, pink

- **Hypericum calycinum**
  Yellow

- **Lantana montevidensis**
  Lavender

- **Liriope spicata**
  Lavender, white

- **Ophiopogon japonicus**
  Lavender

- **Osteospermum fruticosum**
  White, lavender, purple

- **Potentilla tabernaemontanii**
  Yellow

- **Rosmarinus officinalis**
  Blue

- **Santolina**
  Yellow

- **Teucrium chamaedrys**
  Purple, white

- **Trachelospermum jasminoides**
  White

- **Vinca minor**
  Blue, white

Convallaria majalis

Cotoneaster horizontalis

. . . Convallaria majalis

spring, each plant sends up a branching stem bearing the familiar fragrant, bell-shaped, waxy white flowers.

CAUTION: All parts of this plant are poisonous if ingested.

Foliage dies back completely each autumn, then reappears the following spring. Remove dead leaves in late winter or early spring before growth starts, then apply a top dressing of organic matter such as compost or aged manure.

COTONEASTER

Pictured above

Zones: Vary
Type: Evergreen and deciduous
Growth rate: Moderate to fast, to various spreads
Soil: Not particular
Water: Prefers moderate watering; established plants are somewhat drought-tolerant
Exposure: Sun

Cotoneasters are synonymous with easy-care. Their water needs are minimal, they are better left unpruned (except for errant or dead branches), and—

except for occasional susceptibility to fireblight—they're free of pest and disease problems. Numerous cotoneasters make good ground covers; your choices include selected forms and hybrids of about half a dozen species. Though differing in detail, all these plants have small leaves, white or pink single flowers (½ inch wide or less) during spring, and red or reddish berries in autumn or winter.

Deciduous species include *C. adpressus praecox* (Zones 5–10 West, 5–9 East) and *C. horizontalis* (Zones 5–10 West, 5–9 East), with its distinctive herringbone branching pattern. Among evergreens are *C. conspicuus decorus* (Zones 7–10 West, 7–9 East), *C. dammeri* (Zones 5–10 West, 5–9 East), *C.* 'Lowfast' (Zones 7–10 West, 7–9 East), *C. microphyllus* (Zones 6–10 West, 6–9 East), and *C. salicifolius* 'Herbstfeuer' (Zones 7–10 West, 7–9 East).

EUONYMUS FORTUNEI

See Vines, page 54

GAZANIA

See Perennials, page 67

HEDERA

See Vines, page 55

HYPERICUM CALYCINUM

A A R O N ' S   B E A R D

C R E E P I N G   S T .   J O H N S W O R T

Pictured at right

Zones: 6–10
Type: Evergreen to partially deciduous
Growth rate: Fast, to indefinite spread
Soil: Not particular
Water: Prefers moderate watering
Exposure: Sun to shade

Aaron's beard enlarges its territory by underground stems that send up vigorous new growth. This makes it an invasive plant in some situations; but if you can corral its spread, you'll have a tough, good-looking, even ground cover. Each arching stem, reaching up to 1 foot high, bears paired elongated oval leaves up to 4 inches long—rich green in sun, lighter in shade. Five-

petaled, 3-inch yellow blossoms with prominent clusters of stamens appear at stem tips in late spring or early summer.

H. calycinum's dense mat of underground roots and stems easily coexists with surface-rooted trees and shrubs and helps prevent erosion on hillsides. To renew unkempt plantings, cut or mow stems to the ground in winter.

JUNIPERUS

See Shrubs, page 45

LANTANA MONTEVIDENSIS

Pictured on facing page

Zones: 10 and warmest parts of 9
Type: Evergreen
Growth rate: Fast, spreading to 6 feet
Soil: Not particular
Water: Prefers moderate watering
Exposure: Sun

This lantana trails instead of growing upright, but in other respects it's identical to its shrubby relatives (page 77): it bears rough-textured, inch-long leaves and small flowers in tight, nosegaylike clusters. Trailing stems branch freely to make a flat carpet or bank cover; rosy lavender flowers bloom during most or all of the year.

L. montevidensis performs well with a minimum of care in a variety of climates, from seacoast to desert. Old plantings build up a thatch of dead stems beneath

Hypericum calycinum

Lantana montevidensis

Mondo grass is a finer-textured and slower-growing version of its close relative creeping lily turf (*Liriope spicata*, below left). It spreads by underground runners, forming the same sort of grasslike turf; dark green, 8- to 12-inch-long leaves arch over to make a cover about 6 inches high. Spikes of small lavender summer flowers are carried on short stems that are largely hidden by leaves; these are followed by lustrous, beadlike violet-blue fruits.

In warm climates, Mondo grass needs a shady location, but it thrives in sun or shade in cool-summer and coastal areas. To neaten up untidy plantings, mow or cut back in late winter or early spring before new growth begins.

OSTEOSPERMUM FRUTICOSUM

T R A I L I N G   A F R I C A N   D A I S Y

Zones: 9 and 10 (West)
Type: Evergreen
Growth rate: Fast, spreading to 4 feet or more
Soil: Needs good, well-drained soil
Water: Needs moderate watering
Exposure: Sun

On sunny days in late autumn through winter, a planting of trailing African daisies may be covered with a solid sheet of bloom—and even during the rest of the year, you can expect intermittent flowering. The purple-centered, 2- to 3-inch daisies are lavender fading to white, with dark lilac petal undersides; nurseries also offer pure white and solid purple varieties. Growing 6 to 12 inches tall, these plants root wherever their branch nodes touch soil; grayish-green leaves are typically oval and 1 to 4 inches long. Plantings aren't long-lived in the desert but will persist from year to year in other regions. When older

the foliage cover; when this occurs, cut plants back to ground level to renew.

LIRIOPE SPICATA

C R E E P I N G   L I L Y   T U R F

Zones: 4–10
Type: Evergreen
Growth rate: Moderate, to indefinite spread
Soil: Prefers well-drained soil
Water: Prefers regular watering
Exposure: Prefers partial shade

Creeping lily turf does indeed give the effect of a coarse, unclipped turf, with the bonus of pale lavender to white (but unlilylike) flower spikes in summer. Each plant is a clump of very narrow, arching, dark green leaves to 9 inches long; plants spread by underground runners, so separate clumps eventually merge to cover an area in grasslike fashion. Flower spikes grow to about the same height as leaves.

In cool-summer areas, you can grow creeping lily turf in sun; in warmer regions, foliage will yellow unless you plant in partial shade. Where freezing weather or frosts are usual, leaves are likely to yellow during winter. To re-

store a fresh appearance, mow or trim back before growth starts.

OPHIOPOGON JAPONICUS

M O N D O   G R A S S

Zones: 8–10
Type: Evergreen
Growth rate: Slow to moderate, to indefinite spread
Soil: Prefers well-drained soil
Water: Prefers regular watering
Exposure: Partial shade to shade

Fast-growing Ground Covers

Armeria maritima	**Lantana montevidensis**
Baccharis pilularis	**Osteospermum fruticosum**
Cotoneaster	**Potentilla tabernaemontanii**
Gazania	**Vinca minor**
Hypericum calycinum	

. . . Osteospermum fruticosum

plantings become untidy, head back to healthy new growth after the main flowering period is over.

PACHYSANDRA TERMINALIS

JAPANESE SPURGE

Pictured at right

Zones: 4–9
Type: Evergreen
Growth rate: Moderate, to indefinite spread
Soil: Prefers good, acid soil
Water: Needs regular watering
Exposure: Shade to partial shade

Beautiful foliage and an ability to prosper in deep shade, even among shallow-rooted trees, make Japanese spurge an esteemed ground cover. Foliage forms an even, lustrous green carpet that reaches about 10 inches high in shade, up to 6 inches high in partial shade. Oval leaves to 4 inches long are carried in whorls toward the ends of upright stems; plants spread by underground runners, sending up more and more stems as they increase their territory. Spikes of small, fluffy white flowers appear at stem tips in late spring, often followed by small white fruits. Variety 'Variegata', with white-edged leaves, is attractive in shaded locations.

POTENTILLA TABERNAEMONTANII

SPRING CINQUEFOIL

Zones: 4–9 (West), 4–8 (East)
Type: Evergreen
Growth rate: Fast, to indefinite spread
Soil: Not particular
Water: Needs moderate watering
Exposure: Sun to partial shade

Visualize a strawberry plant with yellow blossoms and you'll have a good picture of spring cinquefoil. Like strawberries, these plants spread by runners, forming a 6-inch-high foliage mat that's dense enough when established to crowd out weeds. Each leaf consists of five shiny, toothed leaflets; small clusters of ¼-inch flowers sparkle against leaves in spring and summer, but no fruits are produced. Spring cinquefoil needs partial shade where summers are hot and dry; in cooler areas, it will take full sun. To even up the planting surface, you can mow plants to as low as 2 inches.

Pachysandra terminalis 'Variegata'

ROSMARINUS OFFICINALIS

ROSEMARY

Zones: 7–10 (West), 7–8 (East)
Type: Evergreen
Growth rate: Moderate, to indefinite spread
Soil: Needs well-drained soil
Water: Prefers moderate to infrequent watering
Exposure: Sun

Two named selections of rosemary are low-growing and spreading, good for informal ground covers on sunny,

seldom-watered slopes or level ground. Because the stems root here and there when they contact the soil, one plant soon becomes an ever-enlarging colony.

'Prostratus' has short, needlelike, highly aromatic bright to dark green leaves. Initial growth is horizontal, but secondary stems may arch upward, then curve or twist back toward the ground; they'll trail down the sides of a raised bed. Light gray-blue flowers appear along stems in late winter or early spring. 'Lockwood de Forest' is similar in aspect but has lighter green leaves and brighter blue flowers. Both varieties naturally grow to about 2 feet high if left untrimmed, forming a thick cover with an irregular surface. To limit height or make the surface even, you can shear plantings or selectively cut out branches.

SANTOLINA

Zones: 7–10 (West), 7 and 8 (East)
Type: Evergreen
Growth rate: Moderate, spreading to 3–6 feet
Soil: Not particular
Water: Prefers moderate watering; established plants are drought-tolerant
Exposure: Sun

Consider filling in that sunny patch of infrequently watered garden with one of the *Santolina* species. Lavender cotton, *S. chamaecyparissus*, presents a filmy mass of gray foliage; each very narrow, inch-long leaf is finely divided into feathery segments. The plant spreads outward, its stems arching upward, to form a rather billowy, dense mass; stems root where they touch the soil, extending the spread. In late spring, plants are covered with buttonlike yellow flowers to ½ inch across. *S. virens* has the same growth habit, but its foliage is bright green and its flowers

Shade-loving Ground Covers

Convallaria majalis	**Ophiopogon japonicus**
Euonymus fortunei	**Pachysandra terminalis**
Hedera	**Sarcococca hookerana humilis**
Hypericum calycinum	**Taxus baccata 'Repandens'**
Liriope spicata	**Vinca minor**

Vinca minor

chartreuse. It grows a bit faster than lavender cotton and will tolerate regular watering if soil is well drained.

Both these *Santolina* species may reach up to 2 feet tall but can be kept lower by periodic trimming. If plants start to look ragged, cut them back or shear them in early spring; some gardeners routinely trim plants after flowers fade.

SARCOCOCCA HOOKERANA HUMILIS

Zones: 6–10
Type: Evergreen
Growth rate: Slow, spreading to 8 feet
Soil: Needs good, well-drained soil
Water: Needs regular watering
Exposure: Shade to partial shade

This plant is worth searching out if you want a neat, high ground cover beneath trees or tall shrubs or along shaded pathways. *Sarcococca*'s beauty lies in its thick, glossy foliage—narrow, elegantly pointed, dark green leaves up to 3 inches long. Upright stems reach to 1½ feet, presenting a solid foliage cover; underground runners send up new stems, gradually increasing the spread of an individual plant. In early spring clusters of tiny white flowers are intensely fragrant; small blue-black fruits follow. *Sarcococca* is generally pest-free, but scale is sometimes a problem.

TAXUS BACCATA 'REPANDENS'

See Shrubs, page 49

TEUCRIUM CHAMAEDRYS

GERMANDER

Zones: 6–10 (West), 6–7 (East)
Type: Evergreen
Growth rate: Moderate, spreading to 2–3 feet
Soil: Needs well-drained soil
Water: Prefers moderate watering; established plants are drought-tolerant
Exposure: Sun to partial shade

Germander is a traditional edging plant for herb gardens, frequently clipped into a dwarf hedge. But left entirely to its own devices, it forms a spreading mat with ascending stems (to about 12 inches tall) densely clothed in lustrous, dark green, ¾-inch leaves. In summer, the stem tips carry short spikes of small flowers—rose-purple in one form, white in another. Variety 'Prostratum' makes a ground-hugging carpet with stems rising only 4 to 6 inches high.

The best garden location for germander is a spot in full sun, away from reg-

ular watering. Though you can grow it in partial shade and give it regular watering (provided that drainage is good), growth will be less compact. If a planting becomes untidy, you can shear or mow it to stimulate new branching growth.

TRACHELOSPERMUM JASMINOIDES

See Vines, page 58

VINCA MINOR

DWARF PERIWINKLE

Pictured at left

Zones: 4–10
Type: Evergreen
Growth rate: Fast, to indefinite spread
Soil: Prefers well-drained soil
Water: Needs moderate watering
Exposure: Shade to partial shade

Despite its refined appearance, dwarf periwinkle is one tough customer. It prospers in shade, competes successfully with tree roots, and tolerates erratic watering.

Slender stems, bearing paired dark green, oval leaves to 2 inches long, root at the nodes and tips to increase the plant's spread. Phloxlike, inch-wide, lavender-blue ("periwinkle blue") flowers are scattered over the plant's surface in early spring. Several varieties exist, including selections with variegated foliage, white flowers, and double blue flowers; 'Bowles' Variety' has blossoms larger than those of the basic species.

In cool-summer regions, dwarf periwinkle will grow in full sun as well as in partial to full shade; where summers are hot, plant it in partial shade. Use it by itself or in association with trees or shrubs, since its dense growth will overwhelm most perennials and bulb plants.

Drought-tolerant Ground Covers

Arctostaphylos uva-ursi	Santolina
Baccharis pilularis	Taxus baccata 'Repandens'
Cotoneaster	Teucrium chamaedrys
Rosmarinus officinalis	

Perennials, Bulbs & Annuals Add Bright Color

A bouquet of assets—vivid colors, soft textures, and appealing fragrances—come into your garden when you add flowering perennials, bulbs, and annuals to the scenery. Though a garden design can hold together without these plants, their presence rounds out the picture, adding the extra touch that distinguishes a real garden from an institutional-style landscape.

Providing flower color and handsome foliage, easy-care perennials enhance the garden throughout the growing season, even when not in bloom. Unlike annuals, perennials persist from one year to the next—and most can remain in place for a number of years before needing dividing and replanting.

Bulbs—true bulbs, at least—can't make an all-year contribution to a garden. After the flowering season, their foliage matures and dies, leaving vacant ground for several months. But their exquisite, jewel-like blossoms make bulbs worth including in the landscape—and many bloom in late winter or earliest spring, when little else is in flower.

Annuals do need yearly planting and removal, but they more than compensate for that attention with a long and generous bloom season. Our easy-care choices can be planted in all zones, are generally free of pests and diseases, and require no staking or other fussing. In addition, many of these annuals are content with only moderate watering.

Think of color, and annuals, perennials, and bulbs come to mind. Early spring offers yellow Narcissus *hybrid (top left); summer brings orange butterfly weed (*Asclepias tuberosa, *top center) and variously colored* Portulaca grandiflora *(bottom left). Containers at right provide late spring to early autumn show of white marguerites (*Chrysanthemum frutescens*) and scarlet geraniums (*Pelargonium hortorum*).*

ACHILLEA FILIPENDULINA

F E R N L E A F   Y A R R O W

Zones: 4–10
Type: Evergreen
Growth rate: Fast, to 3–5 feet
Soil: Needs well-drained soil
Water: Prefers moderate watering; established plants are drought-tolerant
Exposure: Sun

A clump or drift of fernleaf yarrow is a garden asset for its foliage alone—but these plants also offer a valuable summer-long display of yellow flowers. Each feather-shaped, medium green to grayish-green leaf is finely divided into ferny segments; a plant's first leaves may be up to 10 inches long, but as flowering stems begin to grow, the leaves along the stems decrease in length. Individual flowers are tiny and petal-less, packed together into flattened heads up to 6 inches across.

Several named selections are widely sold, including 'Coronation Gold' (up to 3 feet tall) and 'Gold Plate' (nearly 5 feet). After flowers fade, they can be cut and dried for arrangements. Crowded clumps decline in vigor after about 4 years; divide plants in early spring.

AGAPANTHUS

L I L Y - O F - T H E - N I L E

Pictured on page 37

Zones: 9 and 10
Type: Evergreen
Growth rate: Fast, to various heights
Soil: Prefers well-drained soil
Water: Prefers regular watering; established plants are drought-tolerant
Exposure: Sun to partial shade

Cool colors are especially valuable in the summer landscape, and lily-of-the-Nile provides them: blossoms come in light to dark blue shades as well as white. Sizes and heights vary among *Agapanthus* species, but all are built along similar lines: fountainlike clumps of strap-shaped foliage, tall flowering stems, and tubular blossoms in open clusters resembling bursts of fireworks.

Nurseries may offer two species—*A. africanus* and *A. orientalis*—and a number of named varieties. You may encounter some confusion of species names: *A. africanus* is sometimes sold as *A. umbellatus*; *A. orientalis* may be labeled *A. umbellatus* or *A. africanus*! Size is the main distinction between the two; *A. africanus* has narrower leaves and

Armeria maritima

stalks to only about 1½ feet tall, while flower stems of *A. orientalis* may reach 4 to 5 feet and bear clusters of up to 100 flowers. *A. africanus* is strictly blue-flowered, but *A. orientalis* offers blue (single or double) or white blooms.

'Peter Pan' is a widely sold dwarf variety, with 1- to 1½-foot bloom stalks rising above foot-high foliage clumps. White-flowered 'Peter Pan Albus' may be the same as 'Rancho White' (also sold as 'Dwarf White' and 'Rancho'); it has 1½- to 2-foot flower stalks and rather broad leaves. Narrow-foliaged 'Queen Anne' bears blue blossoms on 2-foot-tall stems.

For all *Agapanthus* types, select plants in bloom to get the size and flower color you want.

In cool-summer regions, plant lily-of-the-Nile in full sun; in hot-summer areas, locate plants where they will be shaded during the hottest part of the day. Plants need dividing only when they show a definite decline in vigor; early spring is the best time to divide.

ARMERIA MARITIMA

C O M M O N   T H R I F T

Pictured above

Zones: 4–10 (West), 4–9 (East)
Type: Evergreen
Growth rate: Fast, to 1 foot
Soil: Needs well-drained soil
Water: Prefers moderate watering
Exposure: Sun

A good choice for an edging plant, small-scale ground cover, or bright, cheery foreground accent, common thrift looks like a smaller-foliaged, flashier edition of chives. Like chives, it grows in grasslike clumps, but its leaves are shorter and more slender. Each clump sends up many 6- to 10-inch stems topped with rounded clusters of small flowers. Blossoms come in white, or in pink shades ranging from pale pink to deep raspberry; to be certain of color, select plants in bloom.

In mild-summer regions, common thrift flowers almost all year long, but it provides only a long spring display where summers are hot. Foliage clumps spread to about a foot in diameter; divide only when center becomes bare.

ASCLEPIAS TUBEROSA

B U T T E R F L Y   W E E D

Pictured on page 64

Zones: 4–10
Type: Deciduous
Growth rate: Fast, to 3 feet
Soil: Needs well-drained soil
Water: Prefers occasional to moderate watering
Exposure: Sun

The word "weed" accurately indicates this lovely perennial's ease and speed of growth but doesn't do justice to its appearance. In spring, the tap-rooted plant produces a basal clump of foliage, then sends up numerous flowering stems lined with 4-inch, lance-shaped leaves. Stems, reaching 3 feet by midsummer, are topped with showy, flat-topped clusters of tiny, brilliant orange blossoms; the flowers attract butterflies.

This is a "set and forget" perennial for lightly watered parts of the garden. Plants never need dividing and, because of the tap root, should not be moved.

BERGENIA CRASSIFOLIA

W I N T E R - F L O W E R I N G   B E R G E N I A

Zones: 4–10 (West), 4–9 (East)
Type: Evergreen
Growth rate: Slow to fast, to 1½ feet
Soil: Not particular
Water: Prefers regular watering; established plants are drought-tolerant
Exposure: Sun to shade

Handsome, bold-textured foliage and bright flower color in the least colorful season combine in this almost abuse-proof perennial. Throughout the year, its good looks attract attention: the glossy, bright green leaves are thick, rubbery, and prominently veined, shaped like elongated fans to 8 inches across and 10 to 12 inches long. Reddish flowering stems, rising from the foliage in winter or early spring, bear dense clusters of inch-wide single flowers (usually in a shade of pink).

Bergenia grows from thick, branching rootstocks that spread to form dense colonies, good for border plantings, accent clumps, or ground covers. In mild-summer regions, the plant will grow in sun or shade; where summers are hot, it prefers partial to full shade (though sun-wilted leaves have an amazing capacity for recovery). Moderate watering will keep bergenia looking respectable, but growth is faster and more luxuriant with regular watering.

COREOPSIS

Zones: 4–10
Type: Evergreen
Growth rate: Fast, to various heights
Soil: Needs well-drained soil
Water: Needs moderate watering
Exposure: Sun

The yellow, daisylike flowers of coreopsis capture the essence of summer. Throughout the season, the cheery blossoms are carried on wiry stems over bushy mounds of narrow or finely divided leaves. *C. grandiflora* grows 1 to 2 feet high, its blossoms rising airily above clumps of narrow, slightly lobed leaves. The typical flower is bright yellow, 2 to 3 inches across; 'Sunburst' has semidouble blooms, while those of 'Sunray' are semi- to fully double. Foot-tall 'Goldfink' is a good front-of-the-border choice.

Growing 1 to 2½ feet tall, *C. verticillata* blooms from summer through autumn; brilliant yellow single flowers about 2 inches across are carried close to dense mounds of threadlike leaves. Variety 'Moonbeam' features pale yellow blossoms; bright yellow 'Zagreb' is a foot-high foreground specimen.

Coreopsis is unfazed by heat and will thrive despite erratic watering. Performance declines as clumps become crowded; divide in early spring.

GAZANIA

Zones: 9 and 10
Type: Evergreen
Growth rate: Fast, to 1 foot
Soil: Not particular
Water: Needs moderate to occasional watering
Exposure: Sun

Gazanias aren't long-lived perennials, but they grow so quickly and easily and provide so much brilliant color that they're worth replacing or restarting every 3 or 4 years.

The flower is a basic daisy, generally 2 to 3 inches across, available in a wide range of colors and combinations: white, cream, yellow, orange, bronze, red, maroon, and pink. Blossoms often have a dark center or a dark ring at the petal bases. Plants bloom heavily from late spring into summer, but flowers may appear throughout the year in Zone 10.

Gazanias sold in nurseries fall into two groups based on growth habit. Clumping types form tightly knit clusters of plants with long, narrow leaves (sometimes lobed) that are dark green on their upper surfaces, grayish-white

<table>
<tr><td colspan="2">**Spring Perennials**</td></tr>
<tr>
<td>

Armeria maritima
Pink, white

Bergenia crassifolia
Pink

Gazania
White, cream, yellow, orange, bronze, red, maroon, pink

Helleborus
White, pink, purple shades, green

Hemerocallis
Ivory, yellow, orange, red, maroon, apricot, rose, lavender

</td>
<td>

Heuchera sanguinea
Pink, red, white, chartreuse

Iberis sempervirens
White

Lavandula angustifolia
Lavender

Nepeta faassenii
Lavender-blue

Paeonia
White, pink, red, maroon, yellow, cream

</td>
</tr>
</table>

. . . Gazania

beneath. Flowering stems rise above the foliage. Nurseries may offer superior named selections or mixed-color assortments from superior seed strains.

Trailing gazanias, derived from *G. rigens leucolaena,* spread by trailing stems to function as a small-scale ground cover. Foliage is frequently silvery or grayish-green; the range of flower colors is less extensive than that of clumping gazanias. Orange 'Sunburst', yellow 'Sunglow', and green-leafed 'Sunrise Yellow' are three named selections having longer bloom periods and greater resistance to dieback than the older types.

Use clumping gazanias in the garden foreground as accents or color drifts; they'll also serve as a small-scale ground cover on level ground if planted about a foot apart. Trailing types are good for color drifts or ground cover on sloping or level land.

Helleborus orientalis

Heuchera sanguinea

HELLEBORUS

H E L L E B O R E

Pictured at left

Zones: Vary
Type: Evergreen
Growth rate: Slow to moderate, to various heights
Soil: Needs good, well-drained soil
Water: Prefers regular watering
Exposure: Partial shade to shade

Hellebores contribute bold, elegant foliage all year to the shaded patio or woodland landscape. Elongated, toothed leaflets are carried like fingers of a hand at the ends of long leaf stalks; showy five-petaled blossoms resembling single roses bloom in the cooler months.

Two- to 3-inch flowers of Christmas rose, *H. niger* (Zones 4–8), bloom as early as December in warmer zones, in late winter to early spring where winters are colder. Established clumps produce numerous flowering stems, each bearing a single white to greenish-white blossom that turns pinkish purple as it ages. The foliage mass reaches 1 to 1½ feet tall; each glossy, dark green leaf consists of seven to nine narrow, oval leaflets to 9 inches long.

Lenten rose, *H. orientalis* (Zones 4–9), is similar to Christmas rose—but five to 11 broader leaflets make up each leaf. In late winter to early spring, 2- to 3-inch flowers bloom in loose clusters rising above the foliage. Colors include white, pink, green, and purplish shades; blossoms are frequently spotted with dark purple in the center and usually take on green tints as they age.

Shrubby Corsican hellebore, *H. lividus corsicus* (Zones 8–10), grows about 3 feet high. Each light gray-green leaf is divided into three 6- to 8-inch-long leaflets with softly spiny edges. Clusters of 2-inch chartreuse flowers appear at stem tips in late autumn and winter in milder zones, late winter and early spring where the climate is colder.

Consider hellebores permanent plants. They never need dividing and re-establish slowly if moved. Though they grow more lushly with regular watering and a little fertilizer each year, they will persist with no supplementary nutrients and only moderate watering.

HEMEROCALLIS

D A Y L I L Y

Zones: 3–10
Type: Evergreen, semi-evergreen, and deciduous
Growth rate: Moderate to fast, to 1½–5 feet
Soil: Prefers well-drained soil
Water: Prefers regular watering; established plants tolerate moderate watering
Exposure: Sun to partial shade

Attractive foliage, large and lovely blossoms in dazzling colors, ease of growth—daylilies sound almost too good to be true, but they truly are among the simplest and most rewarding perennials to grow. Individual plants resembling young corn plants clump together in fountains of narrow, bright green leaves. Rising above the foliage are slender, branching stems that bear large, lilylike flowers in a range of colors: ivory, yellow shades, orange, red, maroon, apricot, rose, lavender, and various two-color combinations. Flowering starts in midspring and continues for about a month, but you can prolong the season by several weeks simply by selecting both early- and late-blooming varieties. Reblooming types produce a second display in late summer or autumn. As the common name implies, each daylily blossom lasts only a day, but each stem carries numerous buds; some varieties remain open into the evening rather than closing at day's end.

Most modern hybrids reach 2½ to 4 feet tall when in bloom, but you'll also find many miniature hybrids. These are small-scale (1- to 2-foot) versions of the larger lilies, suitable for foreground and border planting.

Daylilies bloom most heavily if planted in full sun, but they'll also perform in partial shade where summers are hot—and actually prefer some shade during the heat of the day in those regions. (Be aware, though, that daylilies planted in shaded spots will face the sun.) Deciduous and semi-evergreen varieties grow in Zones 3 and 4 without the special winter protection that evergreen types need.

Clumps can remain undisturbed for many years, but flower quality is better if you divide them every 5 or 6 years.

HEUCHERA SANGUINEA

C O R A L B E L L S

Pictured on facing page

Zones: 4–10 (West), 4–9 (East)
Type: Evergreen
Growth rate: Moderate, to 1 foot
Soil: Needs good, well-drained soil
Water: Needs regular watering
Exposure: Sun to partial shade

For border and pathway plantings, it's hard to find a more delicate-looking plant than coral bells. Borne atop long leaf stalks, the fuzzy, scallop-edged, heart-shaped to nearly round leaves form mounded clumps that gradually spread as the woody rootstocks branch. From midspring well into summer, wiry 2- to 2½-foot stems rise from the foliage, bearing loose, elongated clusters of small, pendant, bell-shaped flowers that create a bright and airy haze of color. Coral-pink is the most common shade, but you'll also find selections and hybrids with flowers in white, red, other shades of pink, and even chartreuse.

In hot-summer areas, coral bells need partial shade; in other regions, choose a sunny spot. When you notice a decline in vigor (about every 4 years), divide clumps—in spring where winters are cold, in spring or autumn in milder parts of the country.

HIBISCUS MOSCHEUTOS

P E R E N N I A L H I B I S C U S

R O S E - M A L L O W

Zones: 5–9
Type: Deciduous
Growth rate: Fast, to 3–5 feet
Soil: Needs good, well-drained soil
Water: Needs regular watering
Exposure: Sun

Perennial hibiscus blossoms look like old-fashioned hollyhocks, but their great size—6 to 12 inches in diameter—captures the magnificence of tender tropical species.

Vigorous stems begin growth in spring, bearing foliage that may be broadly oval or lobed like maple leaves. Flowers in white, pink shades, or red, sometimes with contrasting centers of deep pink or red, bloom from early to midsummer until frost. Nurseries may offer named varieties in particular colors; seed houses carry strains such as Mallow Marvels and Southern Belle, which will flower 1 to 2 years after planting.

Perennial hibiscus is a permanent plant, never needing dividing or replanting. Set out plants in a protected spot, since summer winds can damage flowers.

HOSTA

P L A N T A I N L I L Y

Zones: 3–9
Type: Deciduous
Growth rate: Slow to moderate, to various heights
Soil: Prefers good, well-drained soil
Water: Needs regular watering
Exposure: Sun to shade

Hosta's summertime blossoms are attractive enough, but they pale in comparison to this plant's leaves. To appreciate the tremendous variety of leaf size, color, and shape among hosta species, hybrids, and named selections, you'll need to visit a nursery or consult a specialty catalog. In general, though, leaves are lance-shaped, heart-shaped, or nearly round, carried at the ends of leaf stalks that radiate from the center of a clump; overlapping layers of leaves give mature plants the look of symmetrical mounds of foliage. Leaves may be smooth or puckery-textured, glossy or dusted with a grayish bloom; color ranges from light and dark green shades to chartreuse, gray, and blue. Numerous color combinations are also possible, including variegations with white, yellow, or cream.

Bell-shaped or lilylike white or lavender flowers are borne on spikes that may barely top the foliage or extend well above it. Overall plant size varies, too—from 6-inch miniatures to those that mound to about 2½ feet high.

Hostas are easy to grow in regions where frosty or freezing winters are followed by humid summers. Where summers are hot, choose a location in partial

---

Summer Perennials

Achillea filipendulina
Yellow

Agapanthus
Blue, white

Asclepias tuberosa
Orange

Coreopsis
Yellow

Gazania
White, cream, yellow, orange, red, pink, maroon, bronze

Heuchera sanguinea
Pink, red, white, chartreuse

Hibiscus moscheutos
White, pink, red

Hosta
White, lavender

Lavandula angustifolia
Lavender

Liriope muscari
Violet

Platycodon grandiflorus
Blue, white, pink

Sedum spectabile
Pink, white

Stokesia laevis
Blue, white

...Hosta

shade, especially if you're planting a variety with considerable white or yellow color. Hostas grown in full sun will be more compact and produce more flowers than those in partial or full shade.

Plants need protection from slugs and snails, especially when new growth emerges in spring. There's no need to dig and divide hostas to keep them vigorous—clumps become more beautiful as they grow larger.

IBERIS SEMPERVIRENS

EVERGREEN CANDYTUFT

Zones: 4–10
Type: Evergreen
Growth rate: Moderate, to 1½ feet
Soil: Needs well-drained soil
Water: Prefers regular watering
Exposure: Sun to partial shade

The common name is "candytuft"—but "snowdrift" better describes the appearance of *I. sempervirens* in full bloom. During mid and late spring, flattened clusters of pure white flowers virtually obscure the glossy evergreen foliage.

Candytuft's low, spreading growth habit makes it suitable for border plantings or a small-scale ground cover. The basic species, its stems covered with narrow leaves up to 1½ inches long, may reach 1 to 1½ feet high and about

Lavandula angustifolia

1½ feet wide. Lower-growing selections include 'Little Gem' and 'Purity'; the superior form 'Snowflake' bears flowers and foliage larger than those of the species and spreads to 3 feet.

Shear off spent flowers after the bloom period is finished to promote a second burst of bloom and enhance the plant's compactness.

LAVANDULA ANGUSTIFOLIA

ENGLISH LAVENDER
Pictured below left

Zones: 6–10 (West), 6–9 (East)
Type: Evergreen
Growth rate: Moderate, to 4 feet
Soil: Needs well-drained soil
Water: Needs moderate watering
Exposure: Sun

With its gray-green foliage and pale violet blossoms, delightfully aromatic lavender adds a welcome cool note to the late spring and summer landscape. The branching, shrubby plant consists of many upward-pointing stems clothed in narrow leaves to 2 inches long. Thin stems grow from branch tips and project well above the plant, carrying 3- to 6-inch spikes of tiny lavender flowers.

The basic species may reach 3 to 4 feet high with equal spread, but nurseries also carry dwarf varieties such as 'Hidcote', with deep purple blossoms; violet-blossomed, midspring-flowering 'Munstead'; and 'Compacta' (under a foot in height).

Lavender prospers in relatively poor soil and prefers only moderate watering, but will succeed with regular watering if soil is especially well drained. To keep plants compact, shear them after flowering (don't cut into leafless stems).

Lavender typically becomes leggy or untidy after about 5 years; when this happens, start new plants from cuttings.

LIRIOPE MUSCARI

BIG BLUE LILY TURF
Pictured above right

Zones: 6–10
Type: Evergreen
Growth rate: Moderate, to 1½ feet
Soil: Needs well-drained soil
Water: Prefers regular watering
Exposure: Partial shade to sun

Generations of southern gardeners have favored big blue lily turf as a border

Liriope muscari

plant for beds and pathways. Today, it's also appreciated as an accent plant, whether set out as individual clumps or planted in small, informal drifts. The dark green, linear leaves resemble coarse grass; growing up to 2 feet long and ½ inch wide, they arch over to make 1½-foot-tall, fountainlike clumps. Flowering spikes appear in midsummer, bearing tight clusters of beadlike violet flowers resembling grape hyacinths; in established clumps, blossoms are partly obscured by foliage. Nurseries offer a number of selected forms, many of which have variegated leaves.

Plants in partial shade will have the best-looking foliage, though a full-sun location can be successful where summers are mild. Big blue lily turf also tolerates deep shade, though its growth is slowed.

Established clumps slowly increase in size but need no periodic dividing. Slugs and snails may damage new leaves in spring.

NEPETA FAASSENII

CATMINT

Zones: 4–10 (West), 4–9 (East)
Type: Evergreen
Growth rate: Fast, to 2 feet
Soil: Needs well-drained soil
Water: Needs moderate watering
Exposure: Sun

Catmint is a classic foreground "filler" plant, spilling over and softening the edges of planting beds. And as the name suggests, cats may find it attractive—though not as enticing as the closely related catnip.

Plants spread to about 2 feet and rise to about that height when in flower. The thin stems are set with small, soft, deeply veined gray-green leaves; in spring and early summer, loose clusters of ½-inch-wide lavender-blue blossoms appear, creating a bluish haze over the plant. To encourage a second bloom period, shear off spent flower stems after the first flush of bloom. If an older plant becomes sparse, cut stems back in early spring or start new plants from cuttings.

PAEONIA

P E O N Y

Pictured at right

Zones: 3–9
Type: Deciduous
Growth rate: Moderate, to 3–4 feet
Soil: Needs good, well-drained soil
Water: Needs regular watering
Exposure: Sun

Hardy and easy to care for, herbaceous peonies have long been considered indispensable perennials by cold-country gardeners. Properly planted in well-prepared soil, a peony will settle in and become increasingly productive as years go by, with no need for division; older plants have been known to outlive the gardens that originally contained them.

The fleshy rootstocks send up numerous stems bearing handsome, deeply divided leaves; each upright to rounded plant is large enough (eventually reaching 3 to 4 feet) to serve as a shrub in the landscape. In mid to late spring, 4- to 10-inch flowers with silky or satiny petals open from round buds carried at the stem tips. Colors include white, cream, light yellow, pink shades, red, and maroon; blossoms may be single (with a tuft of stamens in the center), semi-double, or fully double and pomponlike.

Plant peonies in a spot sheltered from strong winds during the bloom season. If bloom-time weather is consistently hot and dry, also be sure plants get partial shade during the heat of the day.

Peonies are sometimes attacked by botrytis blight; afflicted plants show spots on foliage, and flower buds turn brown and fail to open.

PELARGONIUM

See Annuals, *page 77*

PLATYCODON GRANDIFLORUS

B A L L O O N   F L O W E R

Zones: 3–10 (West), 3–9 (East)
Type: Deciduous
Growth rate: Moderate, to 3 feet
Soil: Needs good, well-drained soil
Water: Needs moderate watering
Exposure: Sun to partial shade

Graceful balloon flower is another "permanent" perennial that, once planted, never needs dividing. It breaks dormancy rather late in spring, sending up branching, 3-foot-tall stems abundantly clothed in oval, olive green, 3-inch leaves. Star-shaped 2-inch blossoms appear in early to midsummer, opening from round, balloonlike buds; if you remove spent blossoms, flowering may continue for about 2 months. The usual flower color is violet-blue, but selections with white or pink flowers are also available. For a front-of-the-border planting that reaches only 1 to 1½ feet high and wide, look for *P. g. mariesii*.

In mild-summer regions, you can plant balloon flower in full sun, but where summer weather is hot (and especially where it's hot and dry), plants need shade during the warmest part of the day.

SEDUM SPECTABILE

Zones: 3–10
Type: Deciduous
Growth rate: Moderate to fast, to 1½ feet
Soil: Needs well-drained soil
Water: Prefers regular watering; established plants tolerate moderate watering
Exposure: Sun

Sedum spectabile offers good-looking foliage during the spring and summer months—and colorful blossoms as an

Shade-loving Perennials

Bergenia crassifolia

Helleborus

Hosta

Liriope muscari

Paeonia officinalis

end-of-season bonus. Dormant clumps begin growth in early spring; stems gradually elongate and fill out with rubbery-textured, sea-green to gray-green, rounded oval leaves, forming dome-shaped or slightly spreading mounds of foliage. In late summer or early autumn, stem tips bear flat-topped 5-inch clusters of tiny flowers. Blossoms are typically pink; for specific shades, choose a named variety.

Plants can remain in place for many years without requiring division. When growth declines in vigor, divide clumps the next spring before growth begins.

STOKESIA LAEVIS

S T O K E S   A S T E R

Zones: 5–10
Type: Evergreen
Growth rate: Fast, to 2 feet
Soil: Needs well-drained soil
Water: Needs regular watering
Exposure: Sun

You'll need to divide overcrowded clumps every 4 years or so, but other than that, Stokes aster requires no special care to produce cool blue or white flowers all summer long. Foliage clumps consist of smooth, lance-shaped green leaves to 8 inches long; leafy, 1½- to 2-foot stems bear small clusters of 3- to 4-inch blossoms resembling both asters and bachelor's buttons. Two widely sold varieties are 'Silver Moon', with blue-tinged white blooms, and 'Blue Danube'.

Ornamental Grasses Offer Graceful Accents

Soft and billowy, perennial ornamental grasses represent the direct opposite of turf grasses. While the ideal lawn has a uniform, monochromatic, putting-green surface, ornamental grasses are favored for their individual forms and colors. Foliage may be green, gray-blue, red-brown, or variegated; some become wheat-colored to rusty brown when cold weather arrives. In many types, flower spikes soar above the leaves in late summer or autumn, bearing plumes or airy heads of tiny flowers.

Ornamental grasses offer no particular gardening challenges. Like most other perennials, they typically prefer well-drained soil and regular to moderate watering. Most do best in full sun, though many will also tolerate partial shade.

Early spring is the best time to plant new clumps; this is also the season to divide and replant older clumps (do so when you see a hollow center where the oldest part of the clump has died out). Give all plantings an annual early-spring grooming: cut back leaves of deciduous species to about 6 inches just as new growth begins; simply remove dead leaves from evergreen clumps.

The grasses described below were selected for individual beauty and good garden manners. None seeds itself prolifically (thus becoming a grassy weed) or spreads aggressively by underground runners.

Calamagrostis acutiflora stricta (feather reed grass), Zones 5–10. Clumps of upright green leaves reach 4 to 5 feet high. Midsummer flower spikes are absolutely vertical to 6 feet, topped with narrow, red-brown flower heads; stems remain intact and upright through winter. 'Karl Foerster' is a bit more open-textured and bushy.

Feather reed grass needs regular watering and will thrive in constantly moist soil.

Festuca (fescue), Zones 4–10. Several fescues make attractive border accents or small-scale ground covers. Familiar *F. ovina glauca* (blue fescue) forms 6- to 12-inch mounds of gray-blue leaves; *F. amethystina* 'April Green' is similar but has bright green foliage. Blue-green *F. a. superba* grows in feathery 1½- to 2-foot clumps and bears thin, somewhat showy flower spikes.

The fescues need partial shade in hot-summer regions and tolerate it elsewhere.

Hakonechloa macra 'Aureola', Zones 4–9. Narrow, arching leaves with bright yellow stripes form mounds up to a foot high; clumps spread slowly by underground runners. This plant prefers partial shade, a cool-summer climate, and good, well-drained, acid soil with regular watering.

Helictotrichon sempervirens (blue oat grass), Zones 5–10. Blue-gray to blue-green leaves in upright clumps give the appearance of a 2- to 3-foot blue fescue.

Miscanthus sinensis (Eulalia grass), Zones 4–10. Fountains of foliage may reach 3 feet high; slender stems up to 6 feet tall bear open sprays of pinkish-tan flowers in late summer or early autumn. Leaves turn golden brown in winter. Variety 'Gracillimus' (maiden grass) has the narrowest leaves; foliage of 'Variegatus' is striped white; leaves of 'Zebrinus' become banded with yellow by mid-summer. All grow well in sun or shade.

Molina caerulea 'Variegata' (purple moor grass), Zones 5–10. Lax, arching leaves striped in creamy white form mounded clumps to 2 feet tall. Cream-colored flower stalks bear pinkish-purple flowers; winter foliage is creamy tan. Plant in full sun, in nonalkaline soil.

Pennisetum, Zones 5–10. Grassy fountains of foliage and foxtail-like flower spikes characterize these pennisetums. Dark green clumps of Chinese pennisetum, *P. alopecuroides*, grow 3 to 4 feet tall; flowers are a silvery pinkish-tan. Variety 'Hameln' grows 1½ to 2 feet tall. Both have yellowish-tan winter foliage. Purple fountain grass, *P. setaceum* 'Cupreum' (Zones 8–10), features 2-foot mounds of red-brown leaves; flower plumes are purplish-red. Neither species is particular about soil; both are drought-tolerant.

Stipa gigantea (giant feather grass), Zones 5–10. Fine-textured, arching foliage in clumps to 3 feet high supports 6- to 7-foot stalks bearing large, open heads of yellowish flowers. Plant in full sun, in good, well-drained soil.

CROCUS

Zones: 3–10
Grows to: 6 inches
Soil: Needs well-drained soil
Water: Needs regular watering
Exposure: Sun

Crocuses are among the first flowers to proclaim that spring is here, though the calendar may still say it's winter.

Dutch crocuses—hybrids of *C. vernus*—have blossoms of white, lavender, purple, yellow, and orange (striped combinations are also sold). Bulb specialists offer various species, including *C. chrysanthus* varieties and hybrids in a range of colors; orange-yellow *C. ancyrensis*, the earliest to flower; and lavender-blue *C. tomasinianus*, which bears its starlike blooms almost as early.

Plant crocuses wherever you'd like to see bright patches of color in a wintry landscape—along pathways, between paving stones, or in drifts beneath deciduous trees. Foliage dies in spring; bulbs will take regular watering if drainage is good, but can remain dry through the summer. Clumps need dividing every 3 or 4 years. Gophers and voles find crocus bulbs appetizing.

ENDYMION

B L U E B E L L

Pictured at right

Zones: Vary
Grows to: 12–20 inches
Soil: Prefers well-drained soil
Water: Needs regular watering
Exposure: Sun to partial shade

"Bell" perfectly describes the shape of *Endymion*'s flowers, but the color isn't always blue. Basic appearance is similar for all species, though: small blossoms are suspended from spikes rising above clumps of strap-shaped leaves.

English bluebell, *E. non-scriptus* (frequently sold as *Scilla nonscripta*), needs at least a bit of winter chill and grows best in Zones 4–9; its slender, ½-inch bells are carried on foot-high, slightly arching stems. Robust Spanish bluebell, *E. hispanicus* (sometimes sold as *Scilla campanulata*), grows in Zones 5–10; upright 1½-foot stems bear ¾-inch bells of blue, pink, or white. Both these species flower in midspring.

Bluebells make beautiful drifts beneath deciduous trees and are also a good choice for accent clumps along

Endymion hispanicus

borders—as long as their yellowing foliage after bloom won't detract from the garden's looks. Plant them in full sun in mild-summer regions, in partial shade in warmer areas. Plants need regular watering from autumn until foliage dies down but prefer little or no water during summer. Divide infrequently; clumps increase in beauty as bulbs multiply.

GALANTHUS

S N O W D R O P

Zones: 3–8
Grows to: 6–12 inches
Soil: Needs good, well-drained soil
Water: Needs regular watering
Exposure: Sun to partial shade

Snowdrops flower so early in the season that it's not unusual to see the blossoms pushing their way up through snow. Flowering stems rise from clumps of strap-shaped leaves, each bearing a single six-petaled, downward-facing blossom at its tip; the three outer petals are distinctly longer and usually tipped in green. Common snowdrop, *G. nivalis*, has inch-long blossoms on 6- to 9-inch stems; giant snowdrop, *G. elwesii*, produces egg-shaped blooms to 1½ inches long on foot-tall stems.

Snowdrops are attractive wherever their delicate, woodland-wildflower beauty can be appreciated early in the year. They prefer full sun until about midspring, partial shade in the warmest months. Though their foliage dies down during summer, bulbs need regular watering during the dormant period. Plantings can remain in place for many years.

LEUCOJUM

S N O W F L A K E

Zones: Vary
Grows to: 6–18 inches
Soil: Needs well-drained soil
Water: Needs regular watering
Exposure: Sun to partial shade

As you might guess from the common name, snowflakes resemble their relatives, snowdrops (*Galanthus*, page 73); leaves are strap-shaped and glossy green, and pendant white blossoms have green petal tips. But snowflake petals are all of equal length and all green-tipped. In the most common species, summer snowflake (*L. aestivum*, Zones 4–10), each 1- to 1½-foot stem bears three to five bell-shaped flowers. Summer snowflake doesn't bloom in summer, though: in mild-winter regions, blossoms may appear from mid-autumn into winter; in colder zones, flowers come in early to midspring.

Blossoms of spring snowflake, *L. vernum* (Zones 4–8), resemble those of summer snowflake but are carried singly atop foot-tall stems.

Snowflakes are attractive in border plantings, naturalized in woodland gardens, or planted in drifts under deciduous trees. They'll grow successfully in partial shade all year or in sun during the bloom period, partial shade during the warmer months. Spring snowflake needs moderate watering in the leafless summer dormant period; summer snowflake accepts moderate watering during dormancy but can also remain dry until autumn. Clumps need division only when flower quality diminishes.

MUSCARI

G R A P E   H Y A C I N T H

Zones: 3–10
Grows to: 8–12 inches
Soil: Needs well-drained soil
Water: Needs regular watering
Exposure: Sun to partial shade

Grape hyacinths provide welcome patches or carpets of blue in the early spring garden. Grasslike leaves emerge in autumn; flower spikes rise from the foliage clumps at bloom time, bearing small, pendant, urn-shaped blossoms resembling tiny grapes. Most popular are selections of *M. armeniacum*; these grow 4 to 8 inches high and produce light or dark blue blossoms, depending on the variety. Italian grape hyacinth,

M. botryoides, reaches 1 foot tall; flower color is typically medium blue, though there is a white variety. Eight-inch spikes of *M. tubergenianum* carry flowers of both light and dark blue, accounting for the common name "Oxford and Cambridge hyacinth."

Use grape hyacinths wherever you want a springtime blue accent—along pathways, under deciduous trees, even between paving stones. Plants need regular watering from autumn through spring, little or no water during summer dormancy. When clumps become crowded, divide bulbs in early autumn.

NARCISSUS

D A F F O D I L

Pictured on page 64

Zones: 3–10
Grows to: 3–18 inches
Soil: Needs well-drained soil
Water: Needs regular watering
Exposure: Sun

Nurseries, garden centers, and mail-order catalogs promote daffodils heavily every year and sell the bulbs in great quantity—so even if you resist the promotions, you're bound to see daffodils come springtime. There are good reasons for their popularity, though; for one thing, they're rewardingly easy to grow. A top-quality bulb will flower the first spring after planting, then continue to bloom year after year with little or no attention. Daffodil specialists (and some well-stocked nurseries) offer a wide assortment of named hybrids in white, yellow, and combinations of white or yellow with pink, orange, or red.

Wintertime Bulbs

■ **Crocus**
White, yellow, orange, lavender, purple

■ **Galanthus**
White

■ **Leucojum**
White

■ **Narcissus**
White, yellow, and white or yellow with orange or pink

In most regions, you should plant bulbs as soon as they're available; in desert areas and where summers are long and hot, delay planting until soil cools in autumn. Choose a location receiving full sun throughout the flowering season, sun or partial shade during the rest of the year. In selecting a planting spot, remember that flowers face the source of light and that foliage dies down after the bloom period.

Water thoroughly at planting time; keep plantings regularly watered (you'll usually be aided by rain or snow) until foliage begins to yellow. From that point until autumn, plantings can remain dry or receive only occasional watering.

Divide clumps only when quantity and quality of blossoms decline; it's easiest to dig and divide just after foliage has died down, when you can see where to dig. Replant bulbs within a month after digging. Watch for slugs and snails from the time leaves break ground until flowering.

SCILLA

S Q U I L L

Zones: Vary
Grows to: 6–12 inches
Soil: Needs good, well-drained soil
Water: Needs regular watering
Exposure: Sun to partial shade

The squills are closely related to bluebells (*Endymion*, page 73) but are easily distinguished by the shape of their flowers—they're starlike, not bell-shaped. In all but one species, blossoms are carried along upright spikes.

Easily grown in Zones 3–8 are *S. bifolia*, *S. siberica* (Siberian squill), and *S. tubergeniana*. Eight-inch stems of *S. bifolia* typically bear turquoise-blue flowers, though there are white, pink, and violet-blue types. Siberian squill usually bears vivid medium blue blooms on its 6-inch stems, but you'll also find varieties in white, pink, and shades of blue. Pale blue flowers in nodding clusters are characteristic of *S. tubergeniana*.

Entirely different from these three species is Peruvian scilla (*S. peruviana*), a native of Mediterranean Europe growing only in Zones 9 and 10. Its foot-high stems are capped with dome-shaped clusters of 50 or more starlike violet-blue flowers. Each bulb produces a fountain-like clump of long, rather floppy leaves.

The three smaller squills can be grown and used as recommended for *Endymion*. Larger Peruvian scilla is effective in small drifts in border plantings.

Catharanthus roseus 'Polka Dot'

BEGONIA SEMPERFLORENS

B E D D I N G   B E G O N I A

W A X   B E G O N I A

Grows to: 6–18 inches
Soil: Needs good, well-drained soil
Water: Needs regular watering
Exposure: Partial shade to shade

Gardeners in Zones 9 and 10 get the maximum enjoyment from bedding begonias: in these mild-winter regions, the plants are perennial and flower for 9 to 12 months of the year. But even in other zones, you can expect a plentiful display lasting from late spring or early summer until frost ends the season.

Bedding begonias are bushy plants with thick, watery stems and thick, glossy, rounded leaves to 2½ inches across; foliage may be bright green, dark green, or—in some strains—bronze or burgundy. The flowers may be single (four-petaled) or fully double in white, pink, red, or combinations of white with pink or red; usual size is about an inch across, but some types feature blooms up to 3 inches wide.

Set out plants after all danger of frost is past—preferably when nighttime temperatures have reached 50°F/10°C or higher. In cool-summer regions, plants will tolerate full sun.

CALENDULA OFFICINALIS

C A L E N D U L A

P O T   M A R I G O L D

Grows to: 1–2½ feet
Soil: Needs well-drained soil
Water: Prefers moderate watering
Exposure: Sun

Calendulas bring warm, summery colors to the garden during the cooler seasons. Where winters are mild (Zones 9 and 10), plants set out in September flower from autumn through winter and on into spring until the arrival of hotter weather. In colder regions, calendulas set out when the growing season begins will bloom throughout spring; those set out in late summer blossom during autumn and frosty weather.

Plants are branching and somewhat bushy, with long, narrow, aromatic leaves that are slightly sticky to the touch. The daisylike flowers, single to fully double and up to 3 inches across,

come in cream, yellow shades, apricot, or orange, sometimes with contrasting dark centers. Nurseries offer numerous named strains varying in color and height; seed houses stock even more.

To thwart attacks of powdery mildew, plant where air circulation is good.

CATHARANTHUS ROSEUS

M A D A G A S C A R   P E R I W I N K L E

Pictured at left

Grows to: 6–24 inches
Soil: Not particular
Water: Prefers moderate watering
Exposure: Sun to partial shade

Sun-worshipping Madagascar periwinkle (often sold as *Vinca rosea*) is one of the "staple" annuals for hot-summer regions, blooming from the onset of summer heat until frost ends the season. Oval green leaves form a glossy backdrop for phloxlike single flowers to 1½ inches across; blossoms are white or pink, sometimes with a red or pink eye. In most strains, the bushy plants grow 1 to 2 feet high, but the Little series is under a foot in height, while the Carpet series is low and spreading, suitable for a small-scale annual ground cover.

Set out plants after all danger of frost is past. Where summers are mild, plant in full sun; in hot-summer areas, choose a location in sun or partial shade (shaded plantings will begin flowering a bit later than those in sun).

CELOSIA

C O C K S C O M B

C H I N E S E   W O O L F L O W E R

Pictured on page 76

Grows to: 9 inches to 3 feet
Soil: Not particular
Water: Prefers moderate watering
Exposure: Sun

You can't overlook a planting of *Celosia:* the brilliant colors demand attention. Of the three flower forms, the plume cockscomb is the most widely grown; flower heads are long, slender, upright feathery plumes in yellow, orange, red, and pink. Chinese woolflower types lack the orderly look of plume cockscomb, instead resembling tangled mops.

The third flower form does, indeed, look like a rooster's comb; crested flower heads are flattened and fan-shaped,

. . . Celosia

with tiny flowers in an elaborately curled, twisted formation across the top of the "comb." Colors include maroon and the bright hues of the plume types.

Both plume and crested cockscombs are available in various named strains, including 2- to 3-foot types as well as dwarf forms. All are upright and bushy, with bright green, pointed oval leaves.

Set out plants well after danger of frost is past. Because they revel in heat, they're not at their best in mild-summer regions. Flowers can be cut at their prime and dried for arrangements.

CHRYSANTHEMUM FRUTESCENS

M A R G U E R I T E

Pictured on page 65

Grows to: 4 feet
Soil: Needs well-drained soil
Water: Needs regular watering
Exposure: Sun

Gardeners in Zone 10 and the warmest parts of Zone 9 know marguerite as a shrubby perennial that will perform for several years before needing replacement. But it serves well in all zones as a fast-growing annual, providing a non-stop succession of daisies on a rounded, bushy plant. The basic species has white or yellow single flowers to 2½ inches across, but nurseries now carry named selections with single, semidouble, or double blossoms in pink as well as white or yellow. The bright green leaves are coarsely divided into many seg-

Celosia

ments; white-flowered 'Silver Anniversary' has finely cut gray-green foliage.

To promote bushiness and increase bloom, pinch or lightly head back plants several times during the growing season. In regions where plants can overwinter, cut back stems more heavily in early spring, but don't prune back to old, leafless stems; these are not likely to produce new growth.

GAILLARDIA PULCHELLA

Grows to: 2 feet
Soil: Needs well-drained soil
Water: Needs moderate watering
Exposure: Sun

The warm autumnal tints of these 2-inch daisies enrich the garden in summer and autumn. You'll often see two different colors arranged in concentric circles around a dark blossom center—a cream edge on red petals or a gold edge on maroon petals, for example. Typical blossoms are single, with fringed petal tips, but some strains produce spherical clusters of tubular flowers. The long, leafless blossom stalks rise above clumps of narrow, hairy leaves; usual height is 1½ to 2 feet, but smaller types grow to only half that size.

Set out plants after danger of frost is past. These long-flowering annuals flourish in hot weather; they aren't at their best where summers are cool.

IMPATIENS

Grows to: 8–24 inches
Soil: Needs good, well-drained soil
Water: Needs regular watering
Exposure: Partial shade to shade

Nothing beats impatiens for brightening shady gardens with plentiful color—and fortunately, nothing could be easier to grow. Common *I. wallerana* (busy Lizzie) bears flowers when plants are just a few inches tall, and the display increases rapidly as plants grow (mature height ranges from 8 inches to 2 feet, depending on the named strain). Each bushy plant is clothed in broadly oval, semiglossy, medium green leaves on light green, succulent stems; circular five-petaled, 1- to 2-inch flowers come in white and dazzling solid or bicolor shades of orange, red, pink, and violet.

New Guinea hybrid impatiens grow 2 feet tall, featuring thicker stems and larger leaves that are usually lance-shaped and may be variegated with ivory, yellow, or red. The 2- to 2½-inch blossoms come in red, orange, pink, lavender, and purple.

Plant impatiens after all danger of frost is past and weather is warm. Except for the New Guinea hybrids, this annual doesn't thrive in full sun, but it does need plenty of light: some sunlight where summers are cool, light shade in warmer regions. Plants are perennial if not killed by frost.

Annuals to Cut

■ **Calendula officinalis**
Orange, apricot, yellow, cream

■ **Celosia**
Yellow, orange, red, pink, maroon

■ **Chrysanthemum frutescens**
Yellow, white

■ **Gaillardia pulchella**
Yellow and red combinations

■ **Tagetes**
White, cream, yellow, orange, red, maroon

LANTANA

Grows to: 2–6 feet
Soil: Not particular
Water: Prefers moderate watering
Exposure: Sun

Lantana flowers lavishly throughout the year if not stopped by frosts—and in Zone 10 and the warmest parts of Zone 9, it's used as a landscape shrub and long-lived container plant. In colder regions, though, gardeners use lantana as an annual source of bright color from summer until frosty weather stops the show. (If you want to save container plants, you can bring them under shelter for the winter, then return them outdoors in spring, as soon as the danger of frost is past.)

In regions where it will grow as a shrub, the original species, *L. camara*, reaches 6 feet high and wide (or even wider). Stems are covered in scratchy hairs; the dark green leaves are similarly rough-textured. The small flowers are grouped in nearly flat-topped, nosegay-like clusters to 2 inches across; innermost flowers are cream to yellow, while the outer ring is pink or orange. Many named selections and hybrids have been developed from this species in a wide range of colors and sizes—from original size down to 2-footers that may spread to two or three times their height.

Lantana thrives in both dry heat and humidity; it's an excellent choice for the seashore, except where persistent fog or clouds encourage mildew. Regular watering and fertilizing will actually cut down on bloom.

LOBELIA ERINUS

L O B E L I A

Grows to: 6 inches
Soil: Needs good soil
Water: Needs regular watering
Exposure: Sun to partial shade

Blossoms in sparkling, jewel-like shades of blue have put lobelia on the summer-garden map. The densely leafy, fine-textured plants are dappled with three-lobed flowers to ¾ inch across; most plants have light to medium green leaves, but 'Crystal Palace'—a long-time favorite selection—has dark bronzy-green foliage as a backdrop for vibrant dark blue blooms. Nurseries also offer varieties with white, pink, crimson, and red-purple blossoms.

Most lobelias have a spreading, mounding habit that makes them a perfect choice for borders and edges of large planters, but selections from the Cascade series are wide-spreading and trailing, well suited for hanging containers.

Lobelia grows in full sun where summer temperatures are mild; in hot-summer regions, it needs partial shade, particularly in the heat of the day. Set out plants after danger of frost is past.

PELARGONIUM

G E R A N I U M

Pictured on page 65

Grows to: 3 feet
Soil: Needs well-drained soil
Water: Prefers moderate watering
Exposure: Sun to partial shade

Geraniums in one form or another are internationally beloved container plants, whether treated as an annual or brought under shelter to survive the winter. In Zone 10 and the warmest parts of Zone 9, they'll persist outdoors for years as shrubby perennials, either potted or in the ground (plants in the open ground may reach a height and width of 5 to 6 feet). Three species are represented by the numerous varieties sold in nurseries.

Familiar *P. hortorum*, the common geranium, has thick green stems and round, scallop-edged, softly furry leaves. Individual single or double flowers up to 1½ inches wide are tightly packed into rounded heads to 6 inches across. There's a wide range of colors: pink shades, red, orange, violet, white, and white with pink or red. If you live in a cold-winter area, it's often easiest to plant one of the seed strains; you can start with seeds or seedling plants and enjoy blossoms throughout summer until first frost without worrying about overwintering plants or cuttings. These strains include a number of dwarf types in the 1- to 2-foot-tall range.

Martha Washington geranium (Lady Washington pelargonium), *P. domesticum*, features 4- to 6-inch clusters of 2-inch, azalealike flowers in pink, red, purple, lavender, and white, generally with velvety patches of darker color in the blossom centers. Carried on woody-looking stems, the stiff leaves are rounded to heart-shaped, with fluted edges. Growth habit is more sprawling than that of common geranium.

Ivy geranium, *P. peltatum*, can be used as a ground cover in Zone 10. In colder regions, plant it in a hanging pot or basket; the lax stems, clothed in thick, glossy, ivy-shaped leaves, will cascade 1 to 2 feet (or more) over the container edges. Single or double, 1-inch-wide flowers in 3- to 4-inch clusters come in pink shades, red, lavender, white, or white with pink or red.

Plant geraniums after all danger of frost is past; choose a partial-shade location where summers are hot and dry. Pinch growing tips from time to time to increase branching and promote compactness. If you overwinter plants, cut them back at least halfway and thin out weak stems just as the growing season begins. Aphids are a potential pest; tobacco budworm and spider mites often appear in midsummer.

PETUNIA HYBRIDA

P E T U N I A

Grows to: 1–2 feet
Soil: Needs well-drained soil
Water: Needs regular water
Exposure: Sun

Petunias are so popular and so widely planted that they scarcely need description. And their popularity is easy to understand: they're unsurpassed for color range, amount of color, and ease of growth in every zone.

Plants are upright to spreading, with thick, oval leaves that are somewhat

---

Annuals with Moderate Water Needs

Calendula officinalis	Lantana
Catharanthus roseus	Pelargonium
Celosia	Portulaca grandiflora
Gaillardia pulchella	Verbena hybrida

. . . Petunia hybrida

sticky and hairy. Lightly fragrant, trumpet-shaped, 2- to 6-inch-wide flowers may be single or double, in red, white, cream, yellow, pink, lavender, blue, purple, and various bicolors.

Nurseries stock numerous petunia varieties and strains, and new ones are introduced almost every year. As a general rule, Multiflora types are smaller-flowered but bloom more profusely than Grandifloras. The two types also differ in growth habit: Multifloras tend to be compact and bushy, while Grandifloras are more spreading (the Cascade series is almost trailing, especially good for hanging containers).

Set out plants in spring after danger of frost is past; in mild-winter desert regions, plant in autumn for spring flowering. When young plants are established, pinch growing tips to encourage branching. If plants become sparse later in summer, you can rejuvenate them by cutting them back halfway.

Tobacco budworm may be a problem from midsummer on. In cool, humid climates, botrytis blight may afflict flowers, then foliage; Multiflora types are more resistant than Grandifloras.

PORTULACA GRANDIFLORA

P O R T U L A C A

R O S E   M O S S

Pictured on page 64

Grows to: 6 inches
Soil: Not particular
Water: Prefers moderate watering; established plants are somewhat drought-tolerant
Exposure: Sun

Extra-easy to grow, willing to reseed itself from year to year, fast-growing and spreading—you might be tempted to call portulaca a weed if it didn't have spectacularly colorful flowers. Plants have succulent, usually reddish-colored stems and slim, cylindrical, succulent leaves up to an inch long. The 2-inch blossoms resemble single to double roses with satiny petals; you'll find them in both brilliant colors and softer shades: yellow, orange, red, fuchsia, pink, cream, white. In most types, flowers open only on sunny days and close in midafternoon—but the Cloud-beater Mixed strain remains open all day, even in overcast weather, while blossoms of Afternoon Delight stay open into early evening.

Set out plants or sow seeds after danger of frost is past. Though portulaca is

Verbena hybrida 'Sangria'

heat-loving and drought-tolerant, it will perform well in cool, moist regions if planted in full sun.

SALVIA SPLENDENS

S C A R L E T   S A G E

Grows to: 1–2½ feet
Soil: Needs good, well-drained soil
Water: Needs regular watering
Exposure: Sun

It's famous for fire engine–red flowers, but scarlet sage is also available in cream, pink, and purple shades that are often easier to work into a garden's color scheme. Bushy plants bear bright to dark green, broadly oval leaves with pointed tips; flower spikes are upright, usually carrying tubular flowers that radiate from the spikes at right angles.

Dwarf varieties such as 'Scarlet Pygmy', 'Blaze of Fire', and 'St. John's Fire' reach about 1 foot high; other varieties and strains achieve heights varying from 1 to 2½ feet. Lower types are effective as border plants; taller kinds make showy clumps or mass plantings. Set out plants after danger of frost is past.

TAGETES

M A R I G O L D

Grows to: 6 inches to 4 feet
Soil: Needs good, well-drained soil
Water: Needs regular watering
Exposure: Sun

Like petunias (page 77), marigolds are one garden flower that's familiar to just about everybody. Plant breeders have had a field day with these annuals, though, so if you think one description covers the field, you're in for a surprise. There's a lot more available than orange pompons on 3-foot plants with finely cut, aromatic leaves.

Hybrid strains of African marigold, *T. erecta,* range in height from 1 to 4 feet; 3- to 5-inch flowers come in white, cream, yellow, and orange. Flower production is prolonged if you remove spent flowers to stop seed formation, but infertile triploid strains—hybrids between African and French marigolds—will flower continuously without deadheading.

French marigold, *T. patula,* includes a number of dwarf varieties. These 6- to 18-inch plants bear single to double blossoms in yellow, orange, or combinations of yellow with red to brownish maroon; typical flowers are about an inch across.

In most regions, marigolds will bloom from late spring or summer until frost; in desert areas, expect the best display in autumn. Set out plants after danger of frost is past.

VERBENA HYBRIDA

G A R D E N   V E R B E N A

Pictured above

Grows to: 6–12 inches
Soil: Prefers well-drained soil
Water: Prefers moderate watering
Exposure: Sun

Colorful garden verbena actually *prefers* rather trying conditions: hot weather, a dry atmosphere, and only moderate amounts of water. Two basic growth habits cover all of the many named varieties and strains: mounding types spread to a limited extent, while definitely spreading types can extend to 3 feet in all directions.

Both mounding and spreading verbenas bear flat, dense, 3-inch clusters of small flowers in white or bright colors—brilliant red, true blue, pink, purple, and lavender—frequently with contrasting white eyes. Narrow, gray-green leaves up to 4 inches long have rough surfaces and scalloped edges.

Set out plants when all danger of frost is past. Garden verbena is a perennial in mild-winter regions, but since it tends to become ragged and untidy in its second year, it's usually treated as an annual. Mildew may be a problem in humid climates and well-watered beds.

Simplify Container Gardening Using Easy-Care Techniques

For portable seasonal color or a small-scale vegetable garden, turn to container gardening. There's some work involved, of course—buying potting soil, filling pots, planting, setting up watering devices. But just as for a full-size garden, you can use easy-care techniques to devise container plantings that won't keep you tied to a tight maintenance schedule.

Containers. Any container you use should have a drainage hole at the bottom. Beyond that, though, you have a wide choice of styles and materials. Pots of unglazed clay (terra cotta) are traditional favorites; their porous sides contribute to soil aeration and help keep the soil temperature down. Clay's porosity also increases evaporation, though, so plants in clay pots require more frequent watering than those in nonporous containers of wood, glazed ceramic, concrete, or plastic.

Container size also determines watering frequency: smaller pots need watering more often than larger ones. For the easy-care gardener, it's obviously simpler to maintain a few large containers than a multitude of small ones.

Soil. Container soil should be light enough for roots to penetrate easily; it should drain quickly enough to prevent roots from becoming waterlogged, yet retain sufficient moisture to keep them from drying out. In nurseries and garden centers, you'll find a number of suitable packaged container soil mixes.

Polymers. For maximum moisture retention, mix your potting soil with superabsorbent polymers. These are gel-like particles that act much like sponges, absorbing hundreds of times their weight in water and dissolved nutrients. Plants can take moisture directly from the polymers; and since polymers retain water that usually drains from the pot, they furnish water after the soil itself is dry.

Water. The easy-care alternative to hand watering is a drip irrigation system (see page 86) with one or more emitters feeding each container. Simply by turning on the water, you can supply all your containers at once. If the emitters are connected to an electric controller, the water can be switched on and off according to a programmed schedule.

Container plantings on a watering system provide seasonal accent color that's both easy to maintain and simple to change.

Fertilizer. Frequent watering rapidly leaches nutrients from container plantings. To ensure healthy plants, apply a controlled- or slow-release fertilizer; with each watering, a small amount of fertilizer will be released into the soil, so plants receive a slow, steady nutrient supply.

Plant choices. Flowering annuals and perennials as well as some vegetables are all suitable container choices. If you're planning a garden of blooming plants, get a headstart on success by choosing easy-care types. And for season-long variety without repeat plantings, combine several plants with different bloom times in one container; for example, try a mix of *Chrysanthemum frutescens* (marguerite), page 76; *Lobelia erinus*, page 77; *Pelargonium hortorum* (common geranium), page 77; *Petunia hybrida*, page 77; and *Tagetes* (marigold), page 78.

Good candidates for a container vegetable garden include tomatoes, beans, summer squash (bush type), peppers, eggplant, lettuce, chard, and even midget corn. For best success, plant your vegetables in the largest container possible to allow maximum root growth. Choose a full-sun location, provide plenty of water, and fertilize regularly.

Installing & Maintaining Your Easy-Care Garden

*I*n Chapter 1, you learned how to choose a garden design perfectly suited to your maintenance goals. You've checked and double-checked your plans—and now you're ready to enter the exciting phase of making those plans a reality.

In installing your garden, just as in developing its design, it's crucial to *think before you act*. Careful preparation of the groundwork and an orderly sequence of building, soil improvement, water systems installation, and planting make installation simpler—and yield a healthy garden that will be easy to maintain for years to come.

On the following pages, you'll find advice and recommendations for garden installation and care, starting with a list of steps to follow as you begin your project. We also discuss soils and soil preparation and review the latest options in time-saving watering systems and devices.

Our tips on care will help assure that your garden is truly easy to maintain. You'll learn the several roles of mulch in an easy-care regime; weed control, plant nutrition, basic defense against pests and diseases, and routine grooming are also addressed.

Finally, on page 94, we include a general review of seasonal maintenance to acquaint you with the rhythms of garden care.

Efficiency garden conserves homeowner energy. Framework of easy-care shrubs and trees is nurtured by a drip irrigation system (black tubing in foreground); seasonal annuals and vegetables that need more frequent attention are confined to narrow raised beds with separate watering systems. Landscape architect: Nancy Hardesty.

Easy Garden Installation

Careful planning is the key to smooth, successful garden installation. Start by establishing the basics: Will you use hired help or not? Where will you buy materials? How much will the project cost? Then move on to scheduling the actual installation tasks.

Labor. If you plan to use hired labor, make sure the services you want will be available when you need them. If you intend to do much of the work yourself, be aware that homeowner labor often requires more time than professional work. Are you prepared to accept a later completion date in exchange for lower costs?

Materials. Before you start the project, know where you'll buy everything you need: structural materials, water system components, plants, and so forth. Find out what you should order in advance and how much notice is required before delivery.

Costs. Total all foreseeable costs, beginning with the expense of removing any parts of the existing landscape (be sure this estimate includes *removal from the site*). Then add up the costs of all new materials: paving and decking, sprinkler parts, soil amendments, and so on (include delivery charges if applicable). If you plan to use designers or contractors, get estimates for their services as well.

Sequence of installation

Set down a sequence of steps for installing the garden, starting at the ground and working upward: removal of unwanted plants and structures, grading the site, structural work (decks, fences, walkways), installation of underground pipes and wires, soil preparation, and finally, planting.

Next, establish a schedule for the project, estimating the time required to complete each step. Ideally, the work should flow smoothly from start to finish; if interruptions are necessary, they should not unduly delay completion. Be guided by your climate and weather, aiming to finish the project at the best time of year for setting out plants.

Clearing the site. Before you begin work, be certain the site is cleared of any elements you don't want in the new garden: unwanted trees or other plants (and their roots), old structures, and any construction debris.

Grading. If major grading is required to alter drainage patterns or improve contours, do it before you begin landscape construction or install watering systems. If, on the other hand, you only need to smooth out small bumps and hollows, you can easily do that with a shovel and rake after other construction is complete.

Construction. After any necessary grading has been completed, proceed to the building of fences, gates, decks, raised beds, retaining walls, and walkways. At this point, it helps to have firm plans for your intended watering system so you'll know where to allow for underground lines. If pipes or wires for timers or outdoor lighting will run underneath walkways or decks, set chase lines below them; later on, you can guide pipes into position through the chase lines.

Watering systems. With all structural work completed, turn to your watering system (see pages 85 to 89). Install underground pipes, sprinkler risers, and any electrical wiring; then fill in trenches and smooth out the soil as necessary. For aboveground water systems, it's better to delay layout and hookup until plants are in place.

Soil preparation. This is the final step before planting. Make sure the soil is free of debris; dig in any amendments necessary to ensure a healthy environment for your plants. For details on soil preparation, refer to page 84.

Soil Types & Soil Preparation

You're confronted by an expanse of bare earth: either the start of a totally new garden or the midpoint in renovating a previous landscape. Before you plant, you'll need to take these steps: determine just what kind of soil you have, clear out the soil, and improve it as necessary.

Knowing your soil

It may look like nothing more than plain old dirt, but ordinary garden soil is, in fact, a complex system of minerals, organic matter, water, air, and microorganisms. The various soil types—sand, clay, and loam—differ in their proportions of these elements. Once you've determined the kind of soil on your property, you'll also be aware of its virtues and limitations; this knowledge, in turn, will influence your choice of plants, let you know what soil improvements are needed, and suggest an appropriate watering schedule.

Basic soil types. Though just three basic soil types are defined, it's unusual to find a garden soil that's purely one type or the other—most have a combi-

Well-organized garden *features a backdrop of easy-care shrubs, trees, and ground covers. Raised bed accommodates annual flowers and vegetables on a drip irrigation system; herbicide keeps gravel path free of weeds. Landscape design: Page Sanders.*

nation of characteristics. Still, you'll probably find that your soil comes closer to matching one of these types than it does the other two.

• *Clay soil* is made up of very fine, flattened particles that pack very closely together, leaving little space for air and water. This dense soil absorbs water slowly and retains it well. Dissolved nutrients also remain in clay longer than in other soils—one reason why many clay soils are quite fertile. To test for a clay or claylike soil, pick up a handful of wet soil and shape it into a ball. Clay will feel slippery; when you let it go, it won't crumble, and if you squeeze it, it will ooze through your fingers in ribbons. When clay soil dries, it becomes crusty and often cracks.

• *Sandy soil* is almost the exact opposite of clay. It's composed of large, rounded particles that pack together about as well as marbles, allowing free passage of water and air. Water enters sand quickly

and percolates through it rapidly, taking dissolved nutrients with it. Consequently, a plant in sandy soil needs supplemental water and nutrients more often than it would if grown in another soil. If you try to squeeze a handful of moist sandy soil into a ball, it will form a cast but barely hold together.

• *Loam soil* represents a balance between the extremes of sand and clay. Loam soils contain large, medium-size, and small particles, plus a quantity of organic matter. Water and air move through the soil slowly enough to keep plant roots moist and nutrients available, but not so sluggishly as in clay soils. A handful of loam will form a pliable ball that breaks apart with a gentle prod.

Acidity & alkalinity. In old-fashioned gardening terms, a soil is sweet (alkaline) or sour (acid). Today, this characteristic is precisely expressed in pH numbers on a scale of 1 to 14, with the midpoint (7) representing neutral. A soil is acid if below pH 7, alkaline (sometimes called *basic*) if above pH 7. Acid soil is the norm in high-rainfall areas; where rainfall is low, soil is typically alkaline.

Some plants—rhododendrons, for example—need acid soil for best growth; a few require alkaline soil, while a number of others will tolerate slight alkalinity. But the majority of popular ornamentals prefer slightly acid to neutral soil (pH 6.5 to 7); extremes of acidity or alkalinity will result in poor growth or even death. For this reason, it's a good idea to know the pH of your soil so you can select appropriate plants. Nurseries and garden centers sell soil test kits that give good readings; if you prefer laboratory testing, contact your county agricultural extension office for information on a soil-testing lab in your area.

If your soil pH tests very high or low, you'll probably need to alter it before you plant. Again, the county agricultural extension can offer advice.

Drainage characteristics. Drainage—the movement of water downward through the soil—is typically rapid in sandy soils, slow in clay. A given amount of water will penetrate about three times deeper in sand than in clay, so it's plain that soil type will influence your watering plans: to moisten a clay soil to the same depth as a sandy one, you'll need to apply about three times as much water.

To get a good picture of your soil's drainage quality, dig a 2-foot-deep hole and fill it with water. When that water has been absorbed, refill the hole; note how long it takes before the water vanishes once again. If water remains in the hole after 6 hours, you can assume that drainage is poor; refer to "Improving drainage" on the facing page for help.

Preparing & improving the soil

Once you've completed the structural work in your garden, you can prepare the soil for planting. The first step is to clear and loosen the soil; after that, amend the soil as necessary, depending on its basic type and on what you want to plant.

Clearing the soil. Even if the soil surface looks neat and tidy, it's still wise to dig or rotary-till the entire area to clear out hidden debris. At a new construction site—particularly if you weren't on hand when the work was done—be on the lookout for buried pieces of wallboard, lumps of plaster, nails, roofing tar, and the like. At the very least, these objects take up space better used by plant roots; at worst, they can interfere with drainage or contaminate the soil. You may also have problems with compacted soil at new sites; if necessary, contact a landscape contractor for soil improvement.

If you're simply redoing an existing garden, construction debris may not be much of a problem,

Runoff problem from sloping land is transformed into a garden feature by two mock streambeds (right and left) that channel excess water. Landscape architect: Nancy Hardesty.

but you'll probably need to get rid of rocks and plant roots. If you've cut down trees or large shrubs, you may need outside help to remove stumps and large root systems.

Amending the soil. Though some soils are naturally better than others, most can still stand some improvement—in the form of extra organic matter and fertilizer—before planting.

• *Organic matter.* Nearly all soils benefit from the addition of organic matter: it renders clay more permeable and sand more retentive, and helps maintain loam in good condition. To put it simply, organic matter improves soil by lodging between soil particles and groups of particles. In clay, particles of organic matter act as wedges, separating the closely packed soil particles and thereby increasing drainage and aeration. In sandy soil, organic matter fills in the larger spaces between particles, allowing the soil to retain more water and dissolved nutrients.

The ongoing breakdown of organic matter by soil microorganisms produces *humus*, a gel-like substance that binds particles together into small units (often referred to as "crumbs"), producing the easy-to-dig condition so characteristic of soils high in organic matter.

No matter what your soil type or what you intend to plant, a good rule of thumb is to incorporate a 3-inch layer of organic matter into the upper 8 to 9 inches of soil. Dig it in by hand—with a spade or fork—or use a rotary tiller. This much organic matter will get the soil into good shape for planting lawns, ground covers, perennials, bulbs, and annuals.

Because of their deep root systems, trees and shrubs benefit from additional preparation in some soils. If you're planting in sand or sandy loam, add approximately one part organic matter to three parts backfill (the soil you return to the planting hole). Heavier loam and clay soils, though, are a different story. It's best simply to dig organic matter *throughout* these soils (as noted above); adding extra organic matter only to the backfill encourages roots to remain within the planting hole, slowing their penetration into the surrounding soil. The planting hole may even become a subterranean "bathtub," absorbing water more rapidly than the surrounding soil and retaining it longer.

• *Types & amounts to use.* There's a wide range of suitable organic amendments to choose from; popular types include nitrogen-stabilized wood by-products (bark, sawdust), peat moss (be sure to moisten it thoroughly before using), mushroom compost, garden compost, animal manures, and a host of regionally available agricultural by-products.

Some amendments are sold prepackaged in bags; a standard 2¼-cubic-foot bag provides a 3-inch depth over 9 square feet. To determine the square footage of the area to be amended, follow these formulas:

> *Rectangular areas:* multiply length by width
> *Triangular areas:* multiply ½ base by height
> *Circular areas:* square the diameter, then multiply that figure by .7854

• *Fertilizers.* Phosphorus and potash, two fertilizers that are most effective when deep in the root zone, should be added at the same time you dig in organic matter. For more on fertilizers, see page 92.

Improving drainage. In descriptions of easy-care plants, you'll often see the phrase "needs well-drained soil." In sand and loam, this requirement is easily met. But deep clay soils present a problem, as do compacted soils and those with a subsurface layer of hardpan. In these cases, you'll need to improve drainage before you can plant.

• *Deep clay soils.* To ensure that plants in deep clay have adequate drainage, plant them in mounds raised above the soil grade by a few inches and liberally amend the soil of the mounds with organic matter. And remember not to overwater: let the top 2 to 3 inches of the soil dry out between waterings.

• *Compacted soil.* Heavy construction equipment can seriously compact soil at new homesites, rendering it poorly drained, difficult to dig, and virtually impossible for plant roots to penetrate. Special soil-loosening equipment may remedy the situation; contact a landscape contractor for possible help.

• *Hardpan.* As its name suggests, hardpan is essentially impenetrable soil. Even if the surface soil is relatively permeable, a layer of dense hardpan beneath it will prevent good drainage. If the hardpan layer is fairly thin, you may be able to dig planting holes to their full width through it into the more porous subsoil; if not to full width, the "chimney" through hardpan should be at least 1 foot in diameter. If the hardpan is too thick for this treatment, your best bet is to plant in raised beds filled with good, porous soil.

Watering Systems

Week in, week out, watering is the garden chore that demands the most consistent attention. And if you have a traditional set-up—that old, familiar garden hose with a hose-end sprinkler—it's an especially time-consuming job as well. You have to move the sprinkler often, dragging it from spot to spot to cover the whole garden, readjusting the flow of water at each new location.

For an easy-care garden, a water-delivery system is a better alternative. Permanent underground lines and semipermanent, aboveground drip irrigation systems will let you position water-delivery heads exactly where you need them for thorough garden coverage; individual systems can water different parts of the yard or a large area. By running the systems with an automatic controller, you'll save even more time.

A well-designed system also conserves water. With careful selection and placement of heads, you can avoid watering areas that don't need it (such as pavements or driveways) and control volume to prevent overwatering and runoff. And low-volume drip irrigation systems can even reduce water loss to evaporation.

Underground systems

Permanent underground sprinkler systems are now more efficient than ever before, thanks to developments in sprinkler head design and refinements in electronic control devices.

Though you may prefer to turn the job over to a professional (see page 8), you can design a system yourself with a little careful planning. Sprinkler manufacturers provide some set-up information for their equipment, but before you buy a complete system, it's important to be sure that your water supply has sufficient capacity to run the system you devise. You'll need to know your water pressure, the volume it will deliver (in gallons per minute), and the delivery rates of the heads you choose.

Materials. To assemble a system, purchase the following components: appropriate fittings to connect the system to your main water supply, an antisiphon control valve (or separate control and antisiphon valves), pipe fittings, risers, and sprinkler heads. For pipes and fittings, the material of choice is polyvinyl chloride (PVC). It won't degrade, it can be cut to length using only a handsaw, and all connections (save those to the main water supply) are made with special PVC solvent cement—so you needn't cut and thread pipes to assemble your system.

Sprinklers. Traditional spray nozzles deliver showers of water in full or partial circles, generally with radii ranging from 6 to 15 feet. Delivery rates vary among the available types, but most apply water quickly—often too fast to be absorbed to the desired depth without runoff, especially on sloping land.

To avoid or minimize runoff, water in a series of short periods, with a brief interval after each period; a controller can regulate the cycle for you. It's also a good idea to purchase matched precipitation-rate nozzles. These guarantee that a half-circle head, for example, will deliver just half as much water as a full-circle head—rather than delivering the same amount over a smaller area.

Another solution to the runoff problem is to use low precipitation-rate nozzles. These supply significantly less water per hour than do traditional spray nozzles; runoff is greatly reduced, since the delivery rate is less likely to exceed the absorption capacity. The familiar impact sprinklers fall into this class, as do single- and multistream rotor types. Both impact and rotor sprinklers disperse a given amount of water over a greater area (up to a 50-foot radius) than do other nozzles.

For watering trees or shrubs with watering basins, you might prefer still another type of nozzle: the bubbler. Bubblers produce a reduced flow of water in a stream, not a spray.

Because an individual sprinkler won't deliver an even amount of water over the area it covers, you must overlap sprinkler spray pattern for even coverage. A workable rule is to separate the heads by half the diameter of their coverage.

If you want to check the actual water dispersal of a particular nozzle, nothing beats the "coffee can test." Place five or more straight-sided cans at measured intervals in a straight line from the sprinkler and run the water for 15 minutes; then measure the water depth in each can. Note the dispersal pattern and adjust the spacing of your sprinkler heads so their overlaps will compensate for uneven delivery.

Drip irrigation systems

A drip irrigation system's key characteristic is *flexibility.* You can tailor the system so each plant is watered by one or more emitters, or you can distribute water over a larger area with microsprayers, minisprinklers, or porous tubing. You can connect your drip system to a hose end for manual control or make a more permanent connection to your main water source; in either case, the system can be run by an automatic controller. And because all drip lines usually are above ground (though they may be concealed with mulch) and made of limber plastic, you can easily change the system's layout and extent, adding or subtracting emitters at will. About the only role drip irrigation isn't suited for is lawn watering—unless the lawn is a small rectangle or narrow strip that can be covered by microsprayers positioned at the perimeter.

All drip irrigation systems operate at low pressure and deliver a lower volume of water than do standard sprinklers. The water is applied slowly at or near ground level, so there's no waste from runoff and little or no loss to evaporation. Emitters are placed so that water is delivered just where the plants need it. The volume of water delivered to each plant is regulated by the number of emitters set per plant and by their delivery capacity in gallons per hour (gph); depth of penetration depends on how long you water.

Assembling the system. A drip irrigation system is remarkably easy to put together. The main feeder line is ½-inch polyethylene tubing. Narrow microtubing ("spaghetti tubing"), just ⅛ to ¼ inch wide, runs from the main line to the plants you want watered; at the end of each length of microtubing, you insert an emitter. There's a full range of connectors—elbows, tees, and so on—made just for assembling the feeder line into more complex configurations. All the tubing is easily cut with scissors or shears; special tools make small holes in the main line for connecting the microtubing. End caps or closure rings close off each feeder line at its end point.

(Continued on page 88)

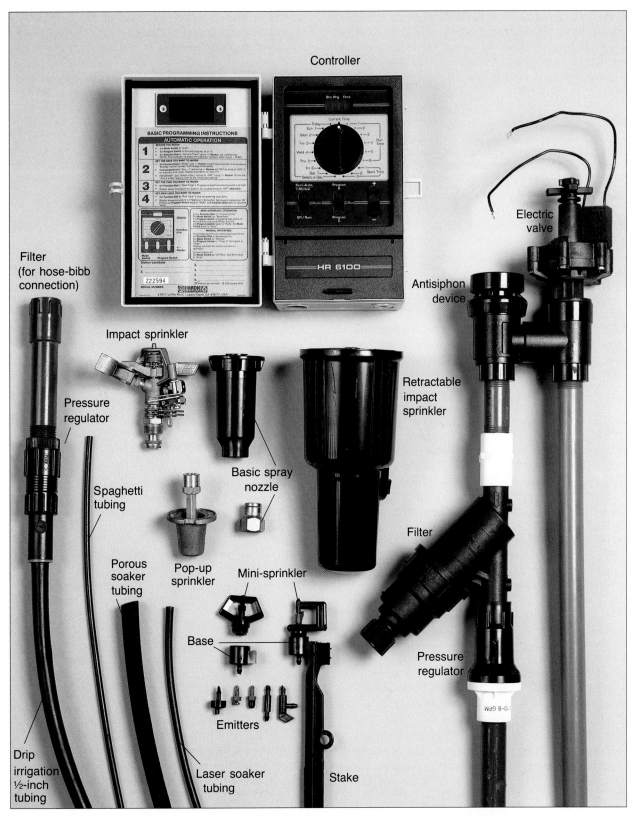

Controller

Filter
(for hose-bibb
connection)

Impact sprinkler

Pressure
regulator

Electric
valve

Antisiphon
device

Retractable
impact
sprinkler

Basic spray
nozzle

Spaghetti
tubing

Porous
soaker
tubing

Pop-up
sprinkler

Mini-sprinkler

Filter

Base

Pressure
regulator

Emitters

Drip
irrigation
½-inch
tubing

Laser soaker
tubing

Stake

Simplify watering by systematizing your garden. Controller (top) operates any system. Assembly of parts (right) and sprinkler heads (center) are components of standard systems; tubing (left) and emitters (center) represent drip irrigation options.

As you devise your system, remember that there are limits to the length of microtubing you can use without pressure loss. Quarter-inch tubing can extend to 10 feet from the main feeder line, but ⅛-inch microtubing can extend only 5 feet.

Hooking up the system. If you connect your system directly to a main water source, install the elements in this order: antisiphon control valve (or separate control and antisiphon valves), filter, and pressure regulator. Beyond this, you'll attach the ½-inch tubing. If you're running a drip system from the end of a hose, the filter and pressure regulator (in that order) will come between the hose bibb and the hose itself. Either type of system can be connected to an automatic controller, but don't use a controller that depends on flow rate for operation.

The filter is definitely critical, no matter how clear you think your water is, since the emitters' tiny openings can easily be clogged by small, undetectable particles carried in the water lines. A pressure regulator is also necessary to maintain the low, steady pressure—usually 20 to 30 pounds per square inch (psi)—needed to ensure proper operation.

Emitters. A number of different emitters are sold, varying in shape and size. But all have the same general purpose: to dispense water slowly to the soil. The flow rate ranges from ½ to about 4 gph.

Standard drip emitters work well on flat or relatively level ground, with lines no longer than 200 feet. But if the lines exceed this length or if the elevation differs by 15 feet or more from one end of the system to the other, gravity or friction will cause a drop in water pressure along the line. In these cases, choose pressure-compensating drip emitters; they can regulate the flow of water so the same amount is delivered throughout the system.

In addition to the standard drip emitter, numerous specialized types are available. Misters and foggers deliver a fine spray, good for increasing humidity around plants such as tuberous begonias. Spitters disperse a low volume of water over a small area; they're favorites for watering container plants.

Microspray and minisprinkler heads are low-volume equivalents of standard sprinkler heads, useful for watering entire beds as long as no obstructions block the spray. Like regular sprinkler heads, they distribute water in full or partial circles but do not deliver it evenly; to ensure even coverage, space the heads so spray patterns overlap. These emitters apply water faster than drip emitters do, at rates of 3 to 40 gph. Some will operate at the same water pressure as drip emitters, but others require higher pressure; if you intend to combine microsprayers or minisprinklers with standard drip emitters, be sure to check the manufacturer's specifications for operating pressure.

Porous tubing. Perforated and soaker tubings are good options for watering plants set out in rows, since they distribute water all along their length. Widely available bi-wall perforated tubing has holes spaced anywhere from 6 to 18 inches apart; it can be buried an inch or two beneath the soil (with holes facing up) or left exposed on the surface. The lighter weight (7-mil) tubing degrades in a year or two on the soil surface; 19-mil tubing lasts for about 5 years. Bi-wall tubing won't bend to go around corners or curves, and gophers find buried tubing quite tasty.

More adaptable than the bi-wall type is flexible perforated tubing with laser-drilled holes; it's available in ¼- and ⅜-inch diameters.

Soaker tubing differs from the perforated kind in that water oozes through the tubing walls rather than through tiny holes. For even application, it must be used on level ground.

In general, both perforated and soaker tubings are designed to operate at about 10 psi—lower pressure than for standard drip emitters. Any of these tubings may become clogged if there's much iron in your water supply.

Automatic devices

The simple addition of electronic controls to your watering system will take it to the top of the easy-care class. No longer need watering be delayed or disrupted due to vacations, late nights at the office, or simple forgetfulness.

Controllers. Hardware stores and suppliers of irrigation equipment offer a variety of electronic controllers ("timers") for home use, ranging from single-program, multiple-station types to complex and versatile multiprogram, multistation systems that can easily handle large gardens with diverse water needs. Most controllers are designed to operate from the typical 110-volt household electrical supply, but you'll also find battery-operated timers that are useful where electrical hookups would be difficult or impossible.

If your plantings have differing water requirements (as most do), look for a dual or multiple-program controller. Each program can be set for a different frequency and length of time; for example, one program might handle lawns, another perennials and ground covers, and a third established shrubs.

Electronic controllers make it easy to avoid runoff problems. You just program the cycles to run for a limited time, several times a day—enough repetitions to ensure that the soil will be moistened to the desired depth, with enough time between repetitions to let water soak in completely.

Sensors & shutoffs. Automatic controllers have one flaw: they operate on a preset schedule that doesn't take weather into account. A timer set to water your lawn every Thursday will do so even if it rains that day or the night before. What's needed is a "weather advisor" for the main control—and two electrical attachments fill the bill.

A *soil moisture sensor* cues the controller to trigger sprinkler operation only when soil moisture is sufficiently low to warrant watering. Such a sensor ensures that watering is less frequent in cool or cloudy weather, more frequent during hot or windy spells. When a moisture sensor is linked to the system, the controller must be set to water every day—but the sensor will trigger it only when water is needed.

Another device that prevents needless watering is the *rain shutoff*. You connect it to the controller, mounting it where it's exposed to open sky but not likely to accumulate leaves or other debris. When rainwater fills the collecting pan to a depth of ¼ inch, an electric impulse shuts off the system. Once the water has evaporated from the pan, the timer is triggered to resume watering according to the preset schedule.

Carpet of river rocks *beneath tree serves as both permanent mulch and distinctive design feature. Landscape design: Garrett Eckbo.*

Easy Garden Care

The routines of garden care vary from one garden to another, but there's one constant: advance planning and intelligent use of maintenance aids can make a big difference in how easily any task is performed. On the following pages, we discuss a few basic ways to streamline garden care.

The virtues of mulch

In general terms, a mulch is a permeable layer of (usually) organic material spread several inches deep over the soil. Good gardeners have long realized its benefits—and in an easy-care garden, it's a crucial part of the low-maintenance regime.

Mulch reduces the rate of evaporation from the moist soil beneath, so you don't need to water as often; it keeps the upper inches of the soil at a cooler, more even temperature, helping surface roots grow steadily. Mulches help prevent both erosion and compaction, since water percolates through the mulch rather than scouring or pounding the soil. And because it effectively buries ground-level seeds, a mulch inhibits weed growth.

An organic mulch offers two further advantages. First, as it breaks down into humus, it improves the soil's structure. And second, it enhances the garden's appearance by providing a neat, uniform carpet beneath plantings.

Organic mulches. Numerous organic materials make successful mulches. Availability, cost, and appearance are your best guides to selection, but you should also keep a few general rules in mind. Avoid thin-textured leaves and other materials that will pack down, preventing or impeding water penetration; for neatness and longevity, choose a mulch that can't easily be blown around or washed away. And if you're mulching a permanent planting, use a material that will last more than one season before requiring replacement.

The mulches listed below all last for at least a year, and all are fairly attractive.

• *Ground bark* from fir, pine, and hemlock trees makes a good-looking, long-lasting mulch with a red-brown color. It's available in different textures, from a fine grind up to 2-inch chunks.

• *Redwood bark* is fibrous, dark red, and durable; coarser-textured *redwood chips* turn from red-brown to gray as they age.

• *Sawdust*, fine-textured and easy to spread, requires nitrogen for decomposition. The commercially packaged product is usually nitrogen-fortified, but raw sawdust should be supplemented

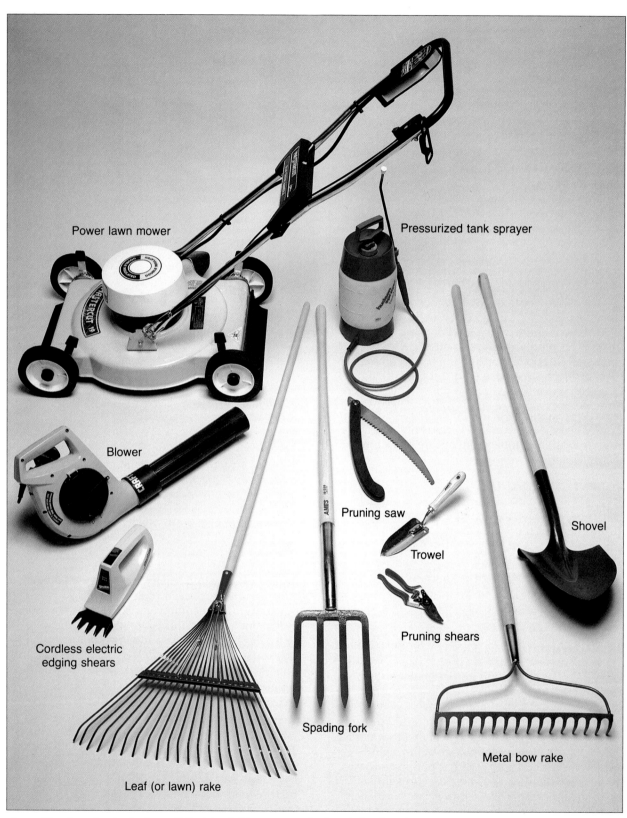

Power lawn mower

Pressurized tank sprayer

Blower

Pruning saw

Trowel

Shovel

Cordless electric
edging shears

Pruning shears

Spading fork

Metal bow rake

Leaf (or lawn) rake

Assembly of garden tools shows all that's needed for easy care. Basic tools for all gardens include lawn rake, spading fork, sprayer, pruning saw and shears, trowel, bow rake, and shovel. Power mower and cordless edging shears simplify lawn grooming, while electric blower is handy for clearing debris from large areas.

with enough fertilizer to provide ½ pound of actual nitrogen for each 100 square feet of 1-inch-deep mulch. (To calculate actual nitrogen, multiply the percentage of nitrogen in the fertilizer by the number of pounds applied—for example, 10 pounds of 5 percent nitrogen fertilizer contain ½ pound of nitrogen.)

• *Straw* is coarse-textured and relatively short-lived, but widely available and easy to handle.

• *Pine needles*, red-brown to gray in color, last for several years. They're unobtrusive and very permeable—and slightly acid, making them a good mulch for acid-loving plants.

• *Grass clippings* make a successful mulch if managed carefully. Spread the clippings in a thin layer, then let them dry before adding a fresh layer; if applied thickly, they'll mat down, becoming slimy, malodorous, and impermeable.

• *Manure* can burn plant roots if it's fresh, so use only well-aged or composted manures.

• *Leaves* tend to blow around more than other materials, but they make a fairly attractive mulch nonetheless. Avoid thin-textured leaves—maple leaves, for example—since these compact when spread in thick layers.

• *Other materials* from local and regional agriculture can be used as mulches. Ground corncobs, apple and grape pomace, hulls of various nut crops, cotton gin trash, and tobacco stems are just a few of the possibilities.

Inorganic mulches. Plastic sheeting, polypropylene fabric, and rocks of varying sizes are all suitable inorganic mulches. Sheeting and fabric offer the bonus of extra-easy installation: you simply roll or spread them out over the ground. They're not attractive, though, so you'll want to cover them with at least a thin layer of a good-looking organic mulch. (Rocks needn't be covered up.)

None of these three inorganic mulches will decompose, so none contributes to soil improvement.

• *Black plastic sheeting*, chiefly used to mulch edible crops set in rows, can be bought in rolls. You cut or punch a hole in the plastic for each plant, or roll plastic strips along both sides of a row of plants. Water reaches the soil only where there's a gap or cutout in the plastic.

• *Polypropylene fabric* allows free passage of water, just as organic mulches do. If protected from sunlight by a layer of organic material, the fabric lasts for many years before degrading. It's particularly useful for erosion control on sloping land.

• *Rocks* can serve as mulches, though they're a far more obvious addition to the garden than most organic mulches. Landscape supply firms sell rocks of varying sizes, shapes, and colors; among the most attractive are river stones, with rounded contours and muted colors. Litter from trees and shrubs won't disappear into a rock mulch, so you'll have to groom rock-mulched beds periodically.

Weed control

You'll never completely banish weeds from your garden; seeds brought in by wind, birds, and muddy feet assure their presence to some extent. Nonetheless, you can keep the weed population in check without breaking your back in the process.

Choose your weapons. There's more than one way to deal with weeds: you can pull them, poison them, or discourage them with mulches. Chances are you'll try all three methods in your easy-care routine. But whatever your plan of attack, the first law of weed control is *vigilance:* eliminate this year's weeds before they produce seeds for next year's crop.

• *Hand methods.* The oldest weed control method involves simply grubbing the offenders out by hand—by hoeing, tilling, or actual hand-pulling. Hand-pulling is an efficient way to eliminate a stray weed or two or even a small patch; hoeing or tilling can effectively clear an area prior to planting. But if you need to get rid of a large number of weeds over a large area, you're better off using an herbicide.

• *Herbicides.* Chemical preparations that eradicate weeds can be a tremendous help if they're used with extreme caution. Be sure to choose the right herbicide for the job; read labels closely and follow directions precisely. If you use these products carelessly, you may seriously damage or kill ornamental plants—or fail to rid your garden of weeds.

Herbicides fall into two general categories. *Preemergence herbicides,* available in granular and concentrated liquid form, kill weed seeds just as they germinate. To be effective, these products must be applied to tilled soil that has been cleared of weeds; after application, you must water the area to encourage germination and activate the herbicide. Preemergents are safe for use among many ornamental plants; check product labels for listings.

• *Postemergence herbicides* eliminate growing weeds; the specific weeds that each product targets are noted on the label. Many of these herbicides were developed to control weeds in grass lawns; others, especially those containing glyphosphate or amino triazole, will eliminate a wide range of plant pests, including woody types such as poison oak and poison ivy.

Postemergents are typically liquid concentrates that you dilute with water, then apply as a spray, though some are sold prediluted in their own applicator containers (these are handy for spot treatments). If you dilute the weed killer yourself, always keep a separate sprayer for it; even a small residue of herbicide can contaminate your other sprays, with potentially damaging results for ornamental plants. And always be sure to spray when the air is still, so the herbicide won't be carried to nontarget plants.

• *Mulches.* As discussed on page 89, a mulch controls weeds by covering their seeds too deeply to allow germination. A mulch is the logical follow-up to any weed eradication campaign, both for future weed control and for the sake of soil improvement and moisture conservation.

Fertilizers

Though rainfall and decomposition of organic matter do provide some nutrients, the quantities supplied are too minute to nurture many favorite ornamentals. For top performance, any garden—whether easy-care or not—requires at least some fertilizing.

Plants vary in their nutrient needs, but in general, those with the highest requirements are the nonwoody plants: annuals, perennials, and lawn grasses. On the other hand, the majority of drought-tolerant plants and many trees and shrubs do well without much fertilizer. Soil type plays a role, too; you can expect to fertilize more often if your garden soil is sandy, since dissolved nutrients leach through sand relatively quickly.

When to fertilize. Almost all lawns will need several fertilizer applications during the growing season to maintain good appearance. Annuals require at least one application—or perhaps more—depending on the type of fertilizer you use (see below). Flowering perennials appreciate fertilizing at the start of the growing season, as do perennial ground covers.

Many easy-care vines, trees, and shrubs will perform quite well with little or no fertilizing, as long as they're growing in loam to claylike soils. However, many gardeners fertilize young trees and shrubs to encourage rapid establishment of roots and promote vigorous growth; once the plants have increased in size, the applications are stopped. Three woody plants, though, perform more successfully with an annual nutrient supplement: *Camellia, Hibiscus syriacus,* and *Rhododendron* (including azaleas).

Types of fertilizer. Most commercial fertilizers are "complete," meaning that they contain the three major plant nutrients: nitrogen (N), phosphorus (P), and potassium (K). The percentage of each element is given as a number on the package label; for example, a 10-5-5 fertilizer contains by volume 10 percent N, 5 percent P, and 5 percent K. For best growth and bloom, a plant needs all three of these nutrients. Remember that phosphorus and potassium (potash) don't leach through the soil efficiently; to do the most good, these elements must be applied at the root zone.

Fertilizers are sold in different forms—liquids, granules, tablets—to be applied in different ways.

• *Liquid fertilizers.* Liquid fertilizer concentrates are diluted with water before being applied to the soil or sprayed onto foliage. Their effect is rapid, but there's scant sustained benefit: dissolved nutrients are leached through the soil with subsequent waterings. As a quick tonic, though, they're unsurpassed.

• *Granular fertilizers.* Dry fertilizer granules dissolve when they contact water; their effects may last from one to several months. Those containing nitrogen in nitrate form act the fastest; nitrogen in ammonium or organic form (and that derived from urea or IBDU) will be released over a longer period.

• *Controlled-release fertilizers.* These are small nutrient pellets with permeable membranes; with each watering, nutrients leach from the pellets into the soil. Depending on the product, nutrients will be released over the course of 3 to 8 months. Controlled-release fertilizers are particularly good for plants in containers, where frequent watering rapidly depletes conventional fertilizers.

• *Sticks, stakes & tablets.* Fertilizers compressed into hard cylinders or large tablets can be pressed or hammered into the soil or placed in holes around the target plants. Water dissolves these products slowly, gradually releasing nutrients for up to a year or more.

• *Combination fertilizers.* Among lawn-care products, you'll find fertilizers that also contain herbicides for weed control, fungicides for disease control, or iron to kill moss. If you need to deal with two tasks at once, these fertilizers can be real time-savers.

Pest & disease control

By selecting pest- and disease-resistant plants, you substantially reduce the potential for problems. You're even less likely to be bothered if you also attempt to clear out favorite overwintering locations for eggs, pupae, and spores; an annual cleanup in late autumn (after leaf fall) to remove dead foliage belongs on every maintenance calendar.

Still, no matter how many precautions you take, some pests or diseases will inevitably appear in your garden from time to time. Be aware that such visits don't always constitute problems: the simple appearance of a pest or disease doesn't mean you must immediately call up the arsenal of deadly controls. Start by identifying the particular insect or disease, then take a good look through the garden to see if it's widespread. Only if the infestation is extensive in the garden or severe on the host plants should you apply the appropriate control.

Whenever you use an insecticide or fungicide spray, water plants thoroughly a day in advance; a water-stressed plant may be damaged by chemical sprays. Avoid spraying when leaves are wet (this dilutes the spray) and during the heat of the day (there's a greater chance for leaf burn). The best times to spray are early morning and late afternoon, when air is likely to be still.

Garden grooming

Because the completely maintenance-free garden does not exist, you'll always have a certain amount of garden grooming and cleanup to do. And though your own garden may contain only easy-care plants, you'll still have to deal with outside influences: the weedy field next door or the neighbor's messy tree that knows no property lines.

If you groom your garden on a regular schedule, you'll enjoy the psychological and aesthetic rewards of a garden that's always neat; you'll also have an easier time keeping up with the job. A weekly investment of 10 minutes—the time it takes to enjoy a cup of coffee—is easier to face (and to schedule) than the once-monthly project of 40 minutes or more.

If you have a lawn, mowing and edging will occupy a major part of your grooming time. Removal of fallen leaves and other garden debris is another ongoing activity, though it's far less time-consuming than lawn care.

Flowering annuals and perennials will look and perform better if you routinely remove spent blossoms; this is seasonal work, dictated by each plant's blooming time. Guidance pruning—trimming occasional wayward branches from trees, shrubs, and ground covers—isn't a job you can schedule; you simply do it when you see the need. The same can be said of weed removal, assuming you've taken the weed prevention measures outlined on page 91.

At the close of the year's most productive period, you should thoroughly clean up spent growth: fallen leaves, dying perennial foliage, exhausted annuals, and the like. When the growing season resumes the following year, you'll need to tidy up in general, prune deciduous trees and shrubs as needed, and replenish mulches.

The few basic grooming tools you'll need are illustrated on page 90. If your garden includes a lawn, you'll also require a lawn mower and an edging tool; power versions of each make maintenance easier and faster. A power blower is useful

Landscape scheme *for minimum maintenance includes a drip irrigation system concealed by moisture-conserving bark mulch. River of rocks follows course of natural garden drainage. Landscape designers: Penny Magrane and Craig Laker.*

for "herding" leaves into piles, but it can't entirely take the place of a leaf rake for finish grooming.

To dispose of debris off the property, you can save time by collecting it in disposable containers. For minor pruning or deadheading, you may need only paper grocery sacks; for more serious cleanup, nothing beats disposable plastic trash bags.

To get a feel for the annual routines of garden care, turn to the seasonal maintenance calendar on page 94.

Plan Your Garden for Seasonal Maintenance

Organized by seasons, this sample maintenance calendar gives you an overview of the annual cycle of garden care and indicates how often some of the more common tasks should be done.

Once your garden is in place, you'll want to set up a more detailed calender than this one, noting weekly chores for each month when garden care is necessary.

Include both ongoing, every-week jobs—mowing and watering, for example—as well as occasional and once-yearly duties such as fertilizing and replanting. The best schedule for your particular garden will depend on the plants you have, your garden design, and, of course, your climate.

Spring

Where winters are mild, spring really begins in late winter; in the coldest regions, some typical springtime events may actually occur in summer. In general, though, these are the springtime activities to schedule.

- Prepare soil as soon as it can be worked.
- If necessary, prune woody plants before growth begins (with the exception of shrubs that flower on wood formed the previous year).
- In cold-winter regions, plant woody plants as soon as ground is workable. In all zones, plant and divide many perennials. Set out annuals and plant seasonal-color containers after all danger of frost is past.
- Replenish mulches.
- Fertilize woody plants and perennials before growth gets underway; begin fertilizing lawns.
- Begin lawn grooming (or continue it, in mild-winter areas).
- Watch for slugs, snails; control as needed.
- Water plantings as needed.

Summer

Lawns grow most rapidly in this season; flowering annuals reach their peak, as do some perennials and shrubs.

- Keep up with lawn grooming: mow and edge weekly.

- Water all plants as needed.
- Fertilize lawns; fertilize annuals and container plantings unless you have used controlled- or slow-release fertilizers that are still effective.
- Keep an eye out for warm-weather pests such as caterpillars, beetles, and spider mites; control as needed.
- Pay attention to miscellaneous garden grooming: tidy up fallen leaves, deadhead spent blooms, eliminate any weeds, and cut out wayward tree and shrub branches before they grow too far.

Autumn

Shorter days foreshadow the end of gardening activities in cold-winter regions but bring a return to planning and planting in mild-winter areas.

- Water as needed; frequency will decrease as days shorten and weather cools.
- Continue lawn grooming unabated in mild-winter regions; elsewhere, continue until growth stops.
- Plant and divide perennials in Zones 7–10.
- Plant bulbs in all zones.
- Plant deciduous trees and shrubs in Zones 6–10; plant evergreen trees and shrubs in Zones 8–10.
- Thoroughly clean up garden debris such as fallen leaves and spent annuals and perennials.
- Watch for slugs, snails; control as needed.

Winter

Where winter cold or snow brings growth to a standstill, outdoor garden work comes to a halt. But in milder regions (especially Zones 9 and 10), there's still periodic work to schedule.

- Water as needed.
- Continue lawn grooming where weather is mild enough to permit lawn growth.
- Plant trees and shrubs now, so their roots will be established before warming weather triggers leaf growth.
- Prune trees, shrubs, vines, and ground covers as needed.
- Prepare soil for spring planting.
- Watch for slugs, snails; control as needed.

Index